History of Scotland

An Enthralling Overview of Important Events and Figures

Free limited time bonus

We forget 90% of everything that we've read in 7 days...

Get the free printable pdf summary of the book you've read AND much, much more... shhhh...

Enter Your Most Frequently Used Email to Get Started

DOWNLOAD FREE PDF SUMMARY

© Enthralling History

Stop for a moment. We have a free bonus set up for you. The problem is this: we forget 90% of everything that we read after 7 days. Crazy fact, right? Here's the solution: we've created a printable, 1-page pdf summary for this book that you're reading now. All you have to do to get your free pdf summary is to go to the following website: **https://livetolearn.lpages.co/enthrallinghistory/**

Or, Scan the QR code!

Once you do, it will be intuitive. Enjoy, and thank you!

Table of Contents

Introduction

East of Edinburgh, along the coastline where the Firth of Forth meets the North Sea, is a small seaside town called North Berwick. In late October 2023, the coast was smashed by huge waves and sea surges. A section of the town's sea wall crumbled from the force, leaving a sixteen-foot-wide gap. Luckily no one was injured, and, apart from the seawall, no property was damaged.

What makes this an interesting moment in Scottish history is that the wall was over four hundred years old. North Berwick, the town, has existed since the thirteenth century. Throughout the Middle Ages, it was the southern station of a ferry used by pilgrims heading to and from the Shrine to Saint Andrew. When New Berwick replaced several water lines, archaeological excavations uncovered hut circles and middens that are at least 2,000 years old. Archaeologists also found Iron Age cist burials, a unique type of stone coffin that can be found at many Scottish sites.

All of this is not to say that North Berwick, despite being a very picturesque town, is extraordinary. Actually, it's the opposite. Scottish history is permanently stamped into the very ground that modern Scotland stands on. History is ubiquitous in Scotland, unescapable from the perspective of someone living in, say, the United States.

Yet, we don't necessarily think of Scotland as an "old" country like Egypt or Greece. Not even, perhaps, as old as England or Spain. This might have something to do with the mighty Roman Empire, which came to Egypt, Greece, Spain, and England but never to Scotland. In the

Romans' view at least, Scotland was never properly "civilized." Scotland, like Ireland, most of Germany, and all of Scandinavia, was *terra incognita* to the empires of the Mediterranean.

Scotland's history might start somewhat obscurely, but over time this relatively small nation became one of the most influential countries in the world. Still, it remains something of a mystery to the outside. This book will peel back the legends to reveal the complex truth lying underneath. It will delve into the past of this nation perched amidst the gray sea and among the crags and heather to expose a history that is not only astonishing but certainly enthralling.

Chapter 1: Ancient Beginnings — Picts, Gaels, and the Formation of Alba

The nation of Scotland is made of the northern third of the island of Britain as well as 790 surrounding islands, which include the archipelagos of the Shetland Islands, Orkney Islands, and the Inner and Outer Hebrides. The geography of Scotland is distinguished by the Highland Boundary Fault, which separates the country into the Lowlands of the east and south and the Highlands of the north and west. The highest mountain is Ben Nevis, which reaches 4,413 feet above sea level.

In the south, the Central Belt, which lies between two large bays called the Firth of Clyde and the Firth of Forth, is home to most of the population, concentrated in the largest city (Glasgow) and the capital (Edinburgh). The northernmost point of Scotland (and the United Kingdom) is Out Stack, an uninhabited island among the Shetland Islands. It is nothing more than a rocky outcrop, but someone traveling north from the island would not meet another landmass before reaching the North Pole.

The longest river is the River Tay, which runs from its source for 120 miles before it empties into the North Sea. Freshwater bodies of water are typically called lochs, with the largest being Loch Lomond. Though Scotland is on the same latitude as Labrador, Canada, its weather is mild thanks to the North Atlantic Drift.

The earliest evidence of humans in the area now called Scotland dates from about 12,000 BCE. These were only a few flint artifacts. More stone tools from a few thousand years later were discovered, indicating that humans began to populate Scotland when the last Ice Age was ending and the glaciers that had previously covered the British Isles were receding. These Mesolithic (Middle Stone Age) people were hunter-gatherers. Gradually, the people of Scotland made significant changes in their modes of living and settlements and became Neolithic (New Stone Age) farmers who deforested land for crops and livestock.

On the main island of the northern Orkney archipelago, two sites point to the existence of incredibly advanced societies in remote locations. First, there is Maeshowe, which was built around 2800 BCE and is a mound burial. Under the mound are tombs and passageways made of crafted flagstone. The most striking element of Maeshowe is the central chamber, which is aligned in such a way that the entire room is illuminated only during the winter solstice. Also on the main island is the site of Skara Brae, a small stone village occupied from 3180 to 2500 BCE. Skara Brae consists of ten clustered houses also made of flagstone with stone hearths, beds, and cupboards. A primitive sewer system featured toilets in each house that flushed into a drain that went into the nearby ocean. Both sites are older than the pyramids of Giza. The inhabitants ate seafood and probably grew barley.

One of the houses, House Eight, lacks beds and cupboards and instead is made of small cubicles. The presence of bones found at that location suggests it might have been a work site for flint tools. Other artifacts found at the site include carved stone balls. These balls, which typically measure about two and three-fourths inches in diameter, have been found all over Scotland and in other places in Britain and Ireland. The exact purpose of these balls is unknown, but they could have been used ceremonially, as weapons, or to move large stone monuments.

One of the key features of these Neolithic sites in Scotland is the presence of cairns. The term "cairn" comes from the Scottish Gaelic word *càrn*. It is a constructed pile of stones used as a marker, sometimes indicating a burial. "Chambered cairns" are burial monuments that consist of a large chamber over which cairns have been placed. Chambered cairns have been found in Ireland, Wales, and England, but the majority are in Scotland, suggesting cultural similarities between these nations. These cairns are often found near Neolithic settlements like Links Noltland, Barnhouse, and Rinyo in the Orkney Islands and Balfarg in the town of Glenrothes. However, neolithic remnants can be found all over Scotland, including the Calanais and Kilmartin Glen standing stones and recumbent stone circles found in the northeast.

Unlike the inhabitants of Skara Brae, most Neolithic Scots lived in wooden houses or huts. These houses, of course, do not remain, so stone sites like Skara Brae or Knap of Howar on Papa Westray are the most prominent examples of Neolithic buildings. Knap of Howar might just be the oldest preserved stone house in Northern Europe and was the site of a homestead. Scots on the Orkney Islands did not have much timber, so they used stones to build, which is why the Orkney Islands seem to have so many Neolithic sites.

On South Ronaldsay in the Orkneys, a farmer digging in 1958 discovered what is now called the Tomb of the Eagles. In it were found 16,000 human bones from at least 324 individuals, as well as talons and bones from twenty birds, predominantly white-tailed sea eagles. Evidence suggests that the tomb was used by Neolithic people for thousands of years.

All these sites suggest that Neolithic Scots were advanced engineers, astronomers, and mathematicians.

Around 2000 BCE, the Stone Age gave way to the Bronze Age in Scotland, and the archaeological record shows a decline in large stone buildings. In the Orkneys, people were buried in smaller *cists*, and the culture of the area was changing. While many of the hallmarks of Neolithic culture spread south from Scotland, Bronze Age culture, denoted by the working of metal, spread north from Europe to Scotland.

One of the earliest Bronze Age finds was discovered when some workmen were blasting a knoll behind Bonar Bridge and found the so-called Migdale Hoard. This collection of jewelry dated from 2000 to 1150 BCE and included a bronze ax head, bronze bangles and anklets, and jet and cannel coal buttons.

At the Forteviot Bronze Age tomb, discovered in 2009, an individual was buried in a *cist* on a bed of quartz and birch bark with a leather bag and a bronze dagger with gold work around the hilt. The tomb dates from between 1950 BCE to 2100 BCE. The site is near Perth, a centrally located city on the River Tay, which has been the site of settlements in prehistoric times, including during the Bronze Age.

A very significant site that dates to about 2000 BCE is at Cladh Hallan on the island of South Uist in the Outer Hebrides. There researchers found four skeletons that had been buried in a peat bog, then removed and stored inside a structure, only to be buried two centuries later. These bodies would have been mummies, preserved around the same time as King Tutankhamun in Egypt. It is particularly interesting and mysterious as to why the bodies were purposely preserved in the bog and then buried hundreds of years later. DNA analysis of the mummies has revealed that they are made of at least six different individuals.

Bronze Age Scots show the first signs of metallurgy and wheeled transport (including chariots). They built large mortar-free or dry-stone structures like brochs, which were usually double-walled stone towers whose exact purpose remains a mystery. They also built Atlantic roundhouses, which were, as the name implies, circular stone buildings with conical thatched roofs. In fact, brochs are considered complex roundhouses as opposed to the simple roundhouses found in Orkney.

These types of structures were carried into the Iron Age, which began in the first millennium BCE. In a field in Stirlingshire in 2009, an amateur metal detectorist discovered the most significant Iron Age metallurgical find in Scotland. It consisted of four golden torcs, a type of necklace that dated from 300 to 100 BCE. It is called the Stirling Hoard. Later investigation revealed that the torcs had been buried inside a roundhouse, perhaps for ceremonial purposes. The torcs exhibit extremely fine craftsmanship, and at least one of the torcs shows a Mediterranean influence in style. This suggests a link between Scotland and Southern Europe, but more evidence is required to substantiate this theory.

The first known written record of Scotland comes from a Greek explorer named Pytheas from the colony of Massalia (Marseille, France). Like many ancient writers, Pytheas' writing does not survive to modern times except when he is mentioned by other, later authors. The exact dates of his voyage into Northern Europe are unknown but are estimated to have been around 350 BCE. Besides seeing Scotland and the British Isles, Pytheas was also the first ancient writer to mention the Arctic and the midnight sun. Pytheas' descriptions of the people of Britain are lacking in detail, mentioning only that they lived in thatched huts, baked bread, and fought from chariots. When he reached the northern part of Scotland, he called the islands Orcas, from which the name Orkney was derived.

By 79 CE, Scotland was said to be the home of the "Caledonii" and the massive, primeval Caledonian Forest found in the writing of Pliny the Elder. This directly resulted from a significant change in Scottish history: the Roman invasion of Britain. The Roman invasion was not just dramatic for the people of Britain but brought the hallmarks of the Roman Empire. Before the arrival of the Romans, Scottish history was told only by archaeological evidence, but after the Romans, written accounts were sent back to Rome, where they were kept for thousands of years. These accounts are always from the Roman perspective and push the Roman agenda, which said that conquest was the right of Rome and beneficial to the conquered. The empire brought civilization, and any resistance to this was a sign of barbarousness and savagery. The ancient Scots, or Caledonians as they were called, certainly appear in Roman writings as savage barbarians.

The invasion of Britain was the brainchild of Emperor Claudius I, who, in 43 CE, needed to show his strength and correct his predecessor's mistake in giving up on an invasion of Britain. The invasion promised glory—and, perhaps more importantly, wealth—to not just the imperial family but the average soldier. The Romans were about 40,000 strong when they landed on the coastline of Southern England. The Romans had some early successes. Claudius landed to take place in the final push of one of the battles and left after sixteen days. He claimed victory, and the Senate awarded him a triumph, calling for triumphal arches to be built and honoring him with the name "Britannicus," though he never used it. Despite Claudius' theatrics, the invasion of England was much longer and harder fought. Still, Britannia became a Roman province and fell under imperial control. However, the land farther north was still unconquered. The Romans traveled into the land they called Caledonia under the command of Gnaeus Julius Agricola, who was responsible for much of the conquest of England.

In 79 CE, the Romans pushed through Scotland quickly with little resistance. However, they failed to inflict heavy casualties on the Caledonians because the natives simply disappeared into the wild forests, or "wilds," as the Romans called them.

Finally, according to the historian Tacitus (Agricola's son-in-law), the Romans met the Caledonian Confederacy in battle at a place called Mons Graupius in northern Scotland in 83 CE. The Caledonians were commanded by a chieftain named Calgacus. These people most likely spoke Scottish Gaelic, a language of the Gaels, an ethnolinguistic group comprising people in Ireland, Scotland, and the Isle of Man. The name Calgacus might have come from the Gaelic word *calgach*, meaning "prickly" or "fierce." This chieftain is the first named Caledonian in history, but he did not last for long. He led his people to defeat at the hands of the Romans. However, Calgacus only appears once in Tacitus' records, where he gives a speech and then is no longer mentioned. This has led some to speculate he was an invention of the writer.

While Agricola certainly dealt the Scots a heavy blow, he did not knock them out, and two-thirds of their army evaded capture in the forests and mountains. Mons Graupius, which might have been in Aberdeenshire, was not the definitive battle Agricola hoped for. His army reached as far as the northern tip of Britain or perhaps no farther than Loch Ness or Moray Firth; it is unclear. Regardless, the Romans eventually turned south, having failed to subjugate the Caledonians. In 85 CE, Agricola was recalled to Rome by Emperor Domitian, who might have been jealous of Agricola's victories. Regardless, Agricola never returned to Britannia.

Several brochs appear to date to the period of Agricola's invasion. In Melrose in the Scottish Borders, Agricola constructed a large Roman fortification. These structures certainly agree with the idea that brochs might have had a military use and that this was a time of invasion and resistance.

A Roman garrison was established in Scotland after Agricola's invasion, totaling 25,000 soldiers. However, Agricola's unknown successor was either unwilling or unable to follow through with the conquest of Caledonia.

Tacitus' description of Agricola's victories is undoubtedly biased and stirring, but he could not conceal the fact that after Agricola's invasion, Scotland remained free and "wild." By 87 CE, just three years after Agricola's victory, Roman forts and camps were dismantled, and the Roman Empire drew back to the Stanegate road between Tyne and Solway Firth, south of the border between Scotland and England.

In 122 CE, the construction of Hadrian's Wall began. The wall was built between Wallsend on River Tyne in the east to Bowness-on-Solway in the west in Northern England. The wall was seventy-three miles long and about eight to ten feet thick in places. It is believed to have been about twelve feet tall.

Emperor Hadrian had wanted to solidify the empire's borders to combat growing revolts and raids from outsiders into Roman-conquered areas. Caledonians, like barbarians elsewhere, would cross into Roman territory (England) to steal and destroy. The intention was that the wall would stop this. According to the archaeological evidence, it succeeded. Very few Roman goods are found in Scotland from this period. Accounts suggest there was a sort of "no-man's-land" beyond the wall that was kept cleared and patrolled by Roman soldiers. No one got in or out. The Caledonians, cut off from their southern neighbors, continued much as they had been while England grew increasingly Rome-like.

The Iron Age Caledonians who lived beyond the wall were farmers and shepherds who grew grain and raised pigs, sheep, and cattle. They settled in small towns or villages, where residents lived in timber buildings with thatched roofs. Higher-ranking families sometimes lived in stone roundhouses or perhaps in brochs. They lived in numerous identifiable tribes ruled by a chieftain, who sometimes had an allegiance to another chieftain, thereby creating confederacies like the one that fought Agricola. They spoke a Brythonic Celtic language and were a Celtic people who worked metal and were excellent horsemen. Their weapons were made of wood, metal, and leather.

According to the Romans, there were sixteen different tribes in Scotland. Twelve of them lived north of the Forth-Clyde isthmus in what is considered Northern Scotland. In later Roman maps, the Caledonii are shown living in the Central Highlands, southwest of a tribe called the Vacomagi. Aberdeenshire was the home of the Taezali tribe, and Fife was the home of the Venicones.

After Hadrian's death in 138 CE, his successor, Antonius Pius, launched a vigorous assault to retake the Lowlands and establish a defensive line below the River Forth. The newly appointed governor of Brittania, Quintus Lollius Urbicus, led the new invasion, and within a few short years, the Lowlands were back under Roman control south of a new imperial line—the Antonine Wall across the Forth-Clyde isthmus. The wall was not built of stone but was an earth rampart with a ditch in front of it. It featured sixteen forts at regular intervals along its forty-mile length, housing 6,000 garrisoned troops. Yet, after ten years, it was briefly abandoned, and ten years later, it was permanently evacuated. After Antonius Pius' death in 161 CE, the northern border shrank back to Hadrian's Wall once again.

Things remained this way until, sometime between 180 and 184 CE, the Caledonians stormed the wall and crossed it. The Romans could not take back the wall, but it was a sign of trouble in the north. By the third century, the Romans faced not only the Caledonians but also another group called Maeatae from territory in Stirlingshire. Both groups appear to have been amalgamations of several smaller tribes that had been absorbed into larger groups, perhaps by force or by alliance.

In 205 or 206 CE, these two groups launched an invasion into Britannia. The governor asked for assistance from the emperor, Septimius Severus, who arrived in 208 CE at the head of a large army. The barbarians waged a guerrilla war but were subdued for a time until the emperor fell ill and died and his son, Caracalla, became emperor. There were plans to try again to take the north by force, but they were abandoned for being unfeasible, and Caracalla made peace with both groups. This was the last attempt by Rome to take Scotland; they would never again attack the people of the highlands and the glens.

However, for the next century, Rome maintained a semblance of order by holding public gatherings in places north of Hadrian's Wall where locals could air their grievances and Romans could keep an eye on any potential troublemakers. These meetings were held at *loci*, which is simply Latin for "places." Each *locus* was held at a place of importance for the natives. The assembly at the *Locus Manavi* (The Place of the Manau district) was gathered around a sacred rock. This name survives in the city and county of Clackmannan, which is Scottish Gaelic for "The Stone of the Manau."

It is not known how often these meetings took place or exactly how they were conducted, but they helped provide a certain amount of peace in the area for generations. Then, in 297 CE, there is mention of two barbarian groups that were particularly troublesome to the Romans. One was the *Hiberni*, who were the inhabitants of the island of Ireland. The others were a group never before mentioned: the *Picti*, or the Picts. Later writings indicate that the Caledonians were the Picts, or it might have been the other way around. Modern historians believe that the Caledonians Confederacy split in two and one group appeared on Roman maps as the *Dicalydones*, a name that indicated the split. The Picts were described by the Roman historian Ammianus Marcellinus in 360 CE as two separate groups: the Dicalydones and another group called the Verturiones. Therefore, the Picts appear to have been a new nation formed from the Caledonian Confederacy and the Verturiones, but the exact nature of this nation is still largely unknown.

The Picts almost certainly didn't call themselves that. Instead, their name for themselves remains unknown. *Picti* was soldier slang for "Painted People," indicating body painting or tattooing. The Romans casually identified anyone north of Firth of Clyde as being Pictish, but it is not clear that these people represented a unified nation or even if they all spoke the Celtic language of Pictish. Still, anyone from the Highlands and the islands of Scotland would have shared certain Pictish characteristics, including body decorations of blue tattoos, religious beliefs, and, most likely, a shared language.

To get a good idea of how widespread the Pictish language was, an excellent source is Claudius Ptolemy's world map, made in about 150 CE. Ptolemy shows the British Isles on the map and gives many tribal names and place names. They were names of Celtic origin given to the Romans, who Latinized them. The massive Isle of Skye is given the name *Scetis* on the map. Linguists believe this was derived from a so-called P-Celtic language, which included Briton and Pictish but excluded Gaelic.

The Pictish language, which is mostly unknown, shared similarities with Welsh, as well. The Welsh prefix "aber," which means "river mouth," can also be seen in Scottish names like Aberdeen and is believed to have been Pictish in origin.

Over the next centuries, the Picts, along with Saxons from Germany and Irish people, attacked Britannia with various levels of success. The Romans, meanwhile, were struggling to hold their empire. In 410 CE, when Britons requested aid from Rome, they were told to fend for themselves. The Roman presence in Britannia was over, and many of the soldiers and citizens, who were already indistinguishable from the Britons around them, simply joined a new era in which British kingdoms arose.

The German Angles, Saxons, and Jutes came to what would be England first as mercenaries and later settled, eventually revolting and pushing the Britons out of their native lands. The Anglo-Saxons, as we call them, called themselves *englisc*, from which is derived "English."

The two tribes who lived in the Lowlands of Scotland, who identified more with the Britons than the Picts, formed their own kingdoms, providing a barrier that kept the Picts in the north. The Votadini tribe became the Gododdin kingdom and built their fortress on Castle Rock in Edinburgh. The Damnonii created a kingdom centered on Dumbarton and what they called Alt Clut or "Clyde Rock" in the Clyde Valley.

This began a period that started in 500 CE or so and is sometimes called the Early Medieval period in Britain. The Roman Empire had left, but their influence was still apparent in the recording of histories in Latin and the spread of Christianity, though both were not embraced by the Picts.

At this time, the Picts were identified as a unified culture and society, though separated into organized kingdoms. They lived in a place called Pictland and erected standing stones, which featured unique symbols and acted as monuments. They were erected by the order of Pictish chieftains, who may now be referred to as kings. These symbols appear on stone at Skye, Perthshire, Orkney, and Shetland with an amazing uniformity. What the symbols meant remains a mystery.

During this Early Medieval period, another kingdom developed—or, more accurately, reemerged—in what is now Argyll on the western coast of Scotland. It was called Dál Riata, and it was not just confined to Scotland but spanned the Northern Channel to Antrim in Northern Ireland. The people of this kingdom spoke Gaelic and were culturally known as Gaels.

The origins of this kingdom are shrouded in legend. Early writers speak of the three sons of Erc, who conquered *Alba*, the Gaelic name for Scotland, but there is little archaeological evidence for an Irish invasion. The people in Argyll were separated from the rest of Scotland by the Highlands, so it is possible they connected culturally with the people of Northern Ireland and created a kingdom founded on this relationship. In fact, modern scholarship and genetic research show that the Scottish Gaels were native to Scotland and not of Irish origin. They were most likely the descendants of the Epidii, a tribe the Romans were aware of in the second century.

The Scottish Gaels were among the first people in Northern Scotland to convert to Christianity after contact with Saint Columba, who crossed from Ireland to convert the peoples of Northern Britain. The Venerable Bede, writing in the eighth century, called the nation of the Gaels *Scottorum*. This is presumably from the Roman custom of calling speakers of Gaelic *Scotti*. From this developed another name for the Gaels of Dál Riata, the "Scots."

The Scots were often at odds with their neighbors, the Picts, and several wars were fought for dominance of the Highlands. The king of Dál Riata, Áed Find (or Áed the White), fought the Pictish king, Ciniod, in 768 CE in the Battle of Fortriu, but the outcome of the battle has since been lost.

Yet, in the final decade of the eighth century, a new group appeared on the shores of Scotland, and they would have a great impact on the Scots and Picts. They were the Vikings. These raiders from Norway appeared to attack at random and disappear, leaving death and destruction behind them. Eventually, it became clear that these were not just raiders but armies of occupation. In 839 CE, the Picts and Scots combined their forces to drive out the invaders, but they were soundly defeated, and the kings of both nations were slain in the battle. This left a vacancy on both thrones. In 840 or 841 CE, the crown of Dál Riata was set on the head of the previous king's son and heir, Cináed mac Ailpin. After a series of short-reigned kings, in 850 CE, the Pictish crown fell to a conqueror who had seized the throne. His name was none other than Cináed mac Ailpin.

Chapter 2: The Emergence of the Scottish Kingdom—MacAlpin to Canmore

Kenneth MacAlpin (also known by the Gaelic name Cináed mac Ailpin) is credited as the unifier of the Scottish Kingdom. The writers of the Irish annals call him *Rex Pictorum*, or "King of the Picts," yet they do not explain how or why he got this title. Historians presumed it was based on the fact that MacAlpin had been a Gaelic conqueror who took control of Pictavia, but this is neither supported nor denied by the documents. It is equally as possible that MacAlpin was a legitimate claimant to the throne of the Picts. The Pictish nobility was known to have contained Gaelic families.

It is not clear whether Kenneth I, as he is sometimes called, united the two kingdoms in 850 CE or much earlier in 842 CE. It was the presence of the Vikings, who raided Pictish and Scottish lands indiscriminately, that drove the two kingdoms together, and MacAlpin, who might have been part-Scot and part-Pict, was the culmination of this merger. He may have put in his bid for the Pictish throne in 842 CE, but the process of defeating his rivals was not complete until 850 CE. At this point he became the first king of a unified kingdom often given the Gaelic name Alba; eventually, it would be known as Scotland. The first kings of the "House of Alpin" were still called "King of the Picts."

KENETH I.

A modern idealized depiction of Kenneth MacAlpin.

One of Kenneth's first actions was to move a collection of relics of Saint Columba (primarily bones) from the island of Iona to the town of Dunkeld in Perthshire just north of the town of Scone. To appreciate the significance of this action, one must understand better who Columba was. Born in Ireland in 521 CE, Columba (or in Gaelic, *Colum Cille*) was the grandson of Irish King Niall. In 563 CE, legend says that he left Ireland as a form of self-imposed exile. A bloody battle had resulted from his refusal to hand over a copy of the Gospels he had supposedly copied illegally. Full of remorse for the deaths he had caused, Columba traveled to the tiny island of Iona because it was out of sight of his native land. There, Columba began building an abbey and is said to have banished snakes, frogs, cows, and women from the island.

Columba was a man of letters and a missionary. His monastery at Iona became the premiere center of learning in the Kingdom of Dál Riata, and he is said to have spread Christianity to the Picts. One of the many miracles attributed to him is the banishing of a "water beast" into the River Ness, which some believe is the first reference to the Loch Ness monster.

Columba, Iona, and the relics associated with the saint became extremely important to the people of Ireland and Scotland. Kenneth's repositioning of the relics to a more central location in his new kingdom shows the beginning of a Scottish national identity. Not all of Columba's relics went to Dunkeld. Some were sent to Ireland, where Columba (or Colum Cille) was also revered.

By the time Kenneth had brought the kingdoms of Dál Riata and Pictavia together, the Irish parts of Dál Riata were their own kingdoms ruled by their own kings. Kenneth's focus was firmly held on the island of Britain. He fought the Britons of the kingdom of Strathclyde, also known as Alt Clut, in the valley of the River Clyde and invaded the region of Lothian in the Kingdom of Northumbria on six separate occasions.

He also had to constantly contend with the Vikings. In fact, he most likely removed the relics at Iona because life on the island was no longer possible with persistent Viking raids. From Iona, he also brought a coronation stone on which the kings of Dál Riata had been crowned and placed it in the royal residence in the town of Scone. It was thereafter known as the Stone of Scone and would be used in the coronation of the kings of Scotland.

Kenneth died in 858 CE, just a few years after securing his new kingdom. According to the Gaelic tradition of "tanistry," the crown then fell to Kenneth's brother, Donald I, also known as Domnall. Donald reigned for just four years before he also died. He was followed by Causantín mac Cináeda, which can be read as Constantine, son of Kenneth. He is often known as Constantine I.

Viking activity was at its height during Constantine's reign. While the "Great Heathen Army" of Vikings were attacking the Anglo-Saxons, the Northumbrians, and the Welsh, other groups of Vikings were attacking farther north from bases they had established in Ireland. Two Viking leaders who might have been brothers, Amlaíb and Auisle, defeated a portion of the Pictish kingdom and obtained tribute and hostages in 866

CE. Later sources claimed that Auisle killed Amlaíb over the former's wife, who was said to be the daughter of Cináeda. However, the accuracy of this story (and whether the wife was the daughter of Kenneth and sister to King Constantine) is completely unknown.

In 877 CE, Constantine was captured and executed by Viking raiders. He was succeeded by his brother Áed, who reigned for less than a year before dying in mysterious circumstances. The next king was Giric, possibly the son of Donald and nephew of Kenneth. He was known as "Mac Rath," or "Son of Fortune." There is scant information on Giric, and it is not clear if he was the King of the Picts alone or the King of Alba. He might have co-ruled with Eochaid ab Rhun, who was also King of Strathclyde and a grandson of Kenneth MacAlpin through his mother. Legend claims that Giric slew Áed, which led to Eochaid's ascent to the throne. It is possible that Giric and Eochaid ruled together or that both claimed the throne of Alba in opposition to each other.

In 889 CE, either Giric died or Eochaid and he were deposed by Domnall mac Causantín, son of Constantine I, who would be nicknamed *Dásachtach*, "the Madman." His name is anglicized as Donald II. He may have been the first king to take the title "King of Alba," or it might have been one of his successors.

By this time, the Picts, decimated by the Vikings, had been won over to Celtic Christianity through missionaries like St. Columba and had abandoned their Brythonic language for Scottish Gaelic. They did not disappear, but outside pressure and time appeared to have forged the Gaels and Picts into the singular Kingdom of Alba. Most historians consider this the end of the process begun by Kenneth and the beginning of what would become the Kingdom of Scotland.

Donald II either died or was deposed by his cousin, Constantine II, grandson of Kenneth and son of Áed, in 900 CE. However, Alba did not extend over all of modern-day Scotland. To the south were the kingdoms of Northumbria and Strathclyde, which were constantly shifting alliances between each other, the English kingdom, and the Welsh. To the north and west of Alba was the Earldom of Sudrland (Sutherland), an old Viking region where the invaders had become largely "Gaelicized."

Map of Scotland in 900 CE.
Eric Gaba, NordNordWest, Uwe Dedering, CC BY-SA 3.0
<https://creativecommons.org/licenses/by-sa/3.0>, via Wikimedia Commons; Labels added by
author; https://commons.wikimedia.org/wiki/File:Scotland_relief_location_map.jpg

Constantine II's reign was largely focused on dealing with incursions from the Vikings, also known as Norsemen. He was, for a time, allied with the growing Kingdom of England in the south. Then, King Athelstan, the first truly English king, invaded southern Alba in 934 CE, though it appears no battles were fought. In retaliation for this invasion, Constantine II allied himself with the King of Dublin and the King of Strathclyde, but they were defeated by King Athelstan in the Battle of Brunanburh in 937 CE, a defining moment in the forging of English national identity.

Constantine II reigned for forty-three years. In 943 CE, he abdicated and joined the Culdees, a monastic and eremitical order in Fife that would come to be associated with the Cathedral of St. Andrew. The Culdees were popular in Ireland and Scotland and were part of the traditions of Celtic Catholicism in which priests were allowed to marry and could engage in business to produce wealth.

He was succeeded by Malcolm I (Máel Coluim mac Domnaill), the son of Donald II. The later chronicles say that Malcolm took an army into Moray and "slew Cellach." It is not clear who Cellach was or if his death resulted in the province of Moray, made from part of the great Pictish kingdom of Fortriu, becoming part of Alba. This seems possible as those in the ruling House of Moray are often described as *mormaers*, a Gaelic name for a regional ruler. Malcolm allied with Edmund I of England and appears to have invaded parts of Strathclyde and Northumbria in conjunction with the Anglo-Saxons. Then, in 954 CE, he was killed either in battle or by the treachery of Moravians in retaliation for his previous invasion.

Malcolm was succeeded by Indulf mac Causantín "the Aggressor," the son of Constantine II. Indulf might have conquered Lothian at this time, bringing the town of Edinburgh into Alba. He died in 962 CE, possibly fighting Vikings. Malcolm I's son, Dub mac Maíl Coluim, then became king.

Dub was known as "the Vehement." He reigned for only five short years and was most likely killed in battle against Cuilén, the son of King Indulf, who wanted the throne for himself. King Cuilén also only reigned for five years before being killed by Britons in 971. His assassin might have been Rhydderch ap Dyfnwal, a Cumbrian who might have been the son of Dyfnwal ab Owain, the King of Strathclyde. According to some accounts, Rhydderch killed Cuilén after the king had raped the Briton's daughter.

The next king of Alba was Amlaíb mac Illuib, another son of King Indulf, but his reign was disputed and short-lived. It seems he lost his bid for the throne and most likely his life to Kenneth II, son of Malcolm I. King Kenneth's nickname is given as "the Fratricidal." The *Chronicles of the Kings of Alba* were compiled during Kenneth II's reign.

The feud that had grown between the two branches of the Alpínid dynasty continued. Kenneth, wanting to secure succession for his descendants, sought to change the rules of succession in Alba. However, this was discovered by his cousin and next in line to the throne, Constantine, son of Cuilén. Before Kenneth could change the laws governing succession, Constantine had him killed by deceit and became the next king, Constantine III, in 995 CE.

Two years later, Constantine III was killed in battle fighting Kenneth III, son of King Dub, who became king in 997 CE and reigned until 1005. King Dub was succeeded by his cousin, the son of Kenneth II, King Malcolm II. In 1018, Malcolm secured Lothia under Scottish rule. In that same year, the King of Strathclyde died, and, thanks to marriage alliances, Malcolm II's grandson, Duncan, sat on the throne of Strathclyde.

In 1034, Duncan succeeded his grandfather as King of Alba, which now stretched south into England. In 1040, Duncan was killed in battle by Maelbeatha, or Macbeth, the *mormaer* of Moray. Despite popular opinion, Macbeth appears to have been a wise monarch who ruled for seventeen years. At this time, Macbeth was defeated in battle by Duncan's elder son, Malcolm III, also known as "Canmore," meaning "Big Head" or "Great Chief."

Malcolm III had grown up in England, and his second wife was the English Princess Margaret, who had taken refuge in Scotland after the Norman invasion of 1066. Margaret tried to lead the Celtic Church of Scotland to the Roman Catholicism of her homeland, where priests practiced vows of celibacy and poverty. Margaret would be canonized for her work by the Catholic Church.

Norman William the Conqueror eventually invaded Scotland and forced Malcolm to pay homage to him. In 1093, Malcolm was killed in battle by a Norman. Malcolm's brother, Donald Bane, claimed the throne but was challenged by Malcolm's son, Duncan. Both were eventually overthrown by an Anglo-Norman force that put Duncan's half-brother, Edgar, on the throne. Edgar was succeeded by his brother Alexander and then by his brother David I, "the Saint."

David did much to improve the lives of the Scots. In a purely medieval sense, he "modernized" what had long been a relatively backwater European kingdom. When he died, the throne passed to a young son, whose reign did not last long. The next king was William "the Lion," who ruled for forty-eight years. At first, he blundered by losing much to the English after a terrible defeat, but eventually, he regained much that he had lost.

The next king was Alexander II, who continued the relatively peaceful and prosperous years of his previous two predecessors. However, Alexander II died in 1249 of illness while attempting to bring the Kingdom of the Isles (the Isle of Man, the Hebrides, and the islands of Clyde) away from their allegiance to Norway. He left behind a seven-year-old son, also named Alexander.

Alexander III, upon becoming an adult, brought the Isle of Man and the Western Isles under Scottish control in 1266 and continued the relative peace and prosperity of his father. He had three children by his first wife, Margaret, daughter of Henry II of England. However, all three children and his wife predeceased him. He declared his granddaughter, Margaret the "Maid of Norway," his successor. He married a second time to Yolande of Dreux, in France. However, he died while riding his horse in a storm in 1286. His new wife was pregnant, but she gave birth to a stillborn child. Thus, the Maid of Norway, a Norwegian princess who was only one year old, was the heir presumptive of Scotland. However, she too died in 1290 on her way to Scotland. This sudden weakness in Scotland's succession proved a perfect opportunity for one of the great villains of Scottish history, King Edward I of England.

Chapter 3: The Struggle for Independence

In Scotland, the news of the Norwegian princess' death caused incredible turmoil. There were now more than a dozen claimants to the throne. The two strongest were Robert de Brus (Bruce) and John de Bailleul (Balliol). Both were of Anglo-Norman origin with estates in England and Scotland. Both were descendants of David I through his youngest son. Both were known by Edward I as they had both served in his army. However, it was believed that Balliol would be the more docile of the two and easily managed by King Edward.

In 1291, with Edward watching, a gathering of nobles announced that Balliol would be given the crown. Edward then immediately demanded that Balliol pay homage to him and recognize England's feudal superiority over Scotland. Balliol would be expected to come to London when called to answer any claims against him and should provide funds for England's defense cost. The new king was also expected to join in a planned invasion of France. Though Balliol might have been as docile as Edward believed, England's demands were too much. Balliol formed an alliance with France and planned to invade England in 1296.

King Edward, called Edward Long Shanks (due to his height of six foot two inches) and "the Hammer of the Scots," was a shrewd king above all else. He had already conquered Wales when he set his sights on Scotland. When he helped facilitate the election of John Balliol as king in what is sometimes called the "Great Cause," he had already decided on a complete conquest of the kingdom. In fact, he had planned for Balliol's refusal of his demands and was prepared to meet the Scottish invasion.

Two days after Balliol entered England, Edward's forces were crossing into the borderlands of Scotland. There, Edward was met by a contingent of Scottish nobles who supported him, many of whom had estates in England, including Balliol's rival Robert Bruce. Balliol took all of Bruce's lands and gave them to his brother-in-law Red John Comyn. Edward marched on Berwick, the most prosperous city in Scotland at the time. He sacked the city and killed many of its inhabitants. Then, at Dunbar, he met and defeated Balliol, who renounced his crown and eventually withdrew to France.

Edward continued, taking Edinburgh, Stirling, Perth, Elgin, and several castles. When he returned to Berwick, a host of nobles and knights signed the "Ragman's Roll" declaring Edward king. Edward left for London, taking the ancient Stone of Scone with him.

Then, in the spring of 1297, a young Scottish knight known as William Wallace got into an altercation with some English soldiers in a marketplace in Lanark. With the help of a girl (some say was his wife), he escaped, but the girl was caught and put to death by the sheriff of Lanark. That night, Wallace returned and killed the sheriff, becoming an outlaw.

People must have seen in Wallace a chance to get revenge against the hated English. Within weeks, he was leading a movement of national resistance. The movement gathered supporters, and in September 1297, an English army under the command of Viceroy John de Warren, Earl of Surrey, faced off against a band of warriors from all over Scotland led by William Wallace. The Battle of Stirling Bridge would become a crucial battle in the First War of Independence and a source of pride for Scots everywhere.

Wallace and his ablest lieutenant, Sir Andrew de Moray, were arrayed on the north bank of the River Forth. The English outnumbered the Scots and were better trained and more experienced. The English army began to cross the Stirling Bridge over the River Forth. This meant that only a small number of English soldiers could face the Scots as the battle began. The Scots used long spears to trap the English cavalry that approached them. Many soldiers and horses tried to cross the Forth but drowned in the muddy waters. The bridge eventually collapsed under the weight of English who could not move forward or back in the confusion. The Scots slaughtered the soldiers remaining on their side while the rest of the army looked on in horror.

The English retreated to Berwick. It was a great victory for Wallace, but Andrew de Moray had been killed in the action. In the summer of 1298, King Edward defeated Wallace at Falkirk, though Wallace escaped. He remained a hunted man until 1303 when he was caught and brutally executed by the English.

It seemed, for a moment, that Scotland would remain subject to the English king, but some nobles were getting restive under English rule. Among them were Robert Bruce, son of the previous claimant to the throne, Red John Comyn, who now led the former Balliol faction, and Sir Simon Fraser of Tweeddale, who had fought alongside William Wallace.

Bruce and Comyn met in Greyfriars Kirk (Church) at Dumfries in 1306. A quarrel broke out, and Bruce stabbed Comyn, killing him. This was not a particularly newsworthy event since rival nobles killed each other often. What made it notable was that the killing had been done in a church and was thus blasphemous. In one act, Bruce had made blood rivals of the Comyns and assured the Catholic Church would oppose his plans to rid Scotland of the English and put himself on the throne.

Despite this, Bruce went to Scone in March 1306, raised the royal standard, and crowned himself the new King of Scotland. In response, Edward sent an English army into Scotland, which defeated Bruce at Methven. Many of Bruce's allies were captured and executed. He went into hiding in the Scottish Islands and possibly Norway. Slowly, Bruce gathered strong allies, including the earls of Lennox and Atholl, Angus Og of Clan Donald, and the powerful Campbell and Maclean clans. He returned to the kingdom and conducted guerilla warfare, achieving victory at Louden Hill.

Edward I decided to lead a great army to subdue the Scots, but, at the age of sixty-eight, died at Burgh-on-Sands in Cumbria, England. England's heir was the king's son, Edward II, but he was not the man to carry on his father's invasion. Edward Longshanks had left his son a kingdom in financial and political difficulties with too many enemies and not enough friends.

The king's death was a turning point for Bruce and Scotland. Robert Bruce defeated his Comyn enemies and was secretly recognized as king of Scotland by the king of France. In 1310, the Church of Scotland decided to support Bruce despite his excommunication by the pope. Bruce invaded and devastated northern England, sacking Durham and Hartlepool. He drove the English garrisons out of Perth, Dundee, Dumfries, Roxburgh, and Edinburgh.

By 1314, Edward II was finally compelled to meet Bruce's army at Stirling, but he made the mistake of letting Robert choose the ground. After a few hours of fighting through marshlands and uphill, the English were fleeing. By 1318, Berwick, the last English stronghold, had fallen and the Scots were again free from English rule.

Edward II tried to invade Scotland again in 1322, but he was chased back into Yorkshire so rapidly that he didn't have time to gather his baggage. Edward tried to get the new pope, John XXII, to confirm the excommunication of Robert Bruce. This caused the Scottish nobles to address themselves to the pope directly. "We fight," they told him, "not for glory, nor riches, nor honor, but only for that liberty which no true man relinquishes but with his life." The Pope appears to have been somewhat swayed as he lifted Bruce's excommunication.

In 1327, Edward II was deposed by his wife, and his young son, Edward III, took his place on England's throne. A peace treaty, the Treaty of Edinburgh-Northampton, was signed between the two kingdoms in 1328. In it, England recognized Scotland as a separate kingdom and Robert Bruce as the rightful king.

By this time, the kings of Alba had long been using a different title, but the exact time the change was made is unclear. By the reign of David I in 1124, the ruler was known as *Rex Scottorum* or "King of the Scots," but this was sometimes written as *Rex Scotiae,* or "King of Scotland."

King Robert I had ruled as King of the Scots—focusing on the people instead of the land—since 1306, but the English did not recognize him as such until 1328. He did not live long enough to enjoy the new peace. In June 1329, Robert I, who had fought so hard to free Scotland and had been suffering from a serious disease (possibly leprosy), died at the Manor of Cardross near Dumbarton. His five-year-old son, already married to the English Princess Joan, became King David II. King Robert's daughter, Margery, had married a nobleman named Walter FitzAlan, the Hereditary High Steward of Scotland. This brother-in-law of the new king was often known as Walter Stewart or, in later forms, Stuart. The regent was Bruce's nephew, Thomas Randolph, Earl of

Moray.

When a group of disgruntled Scottish nobles, urged on by Edward III, landed at Fife with the intent of putting John Balliol (Toom Tabard)'s son, Edward Balliol, on the Scottish throne, Randolph went to meet them but died before the battle commenced.

The next regent was another of Bruce's nephews, the Earl of Mar, who was defeated and killed in a night attack. The invaders marched to Scone, where they crowned Balliol. Before the usurper could do much damage, an army led by Archibald Douglas and Andrew Moray of Bothwell drove him out of the kingdom.

Edward III took this moment to strike and marched to retake Berwick, which he did. Scottish nobles switched sides and allied with the English, and the Lowlands were taken once again. David II was forced to flee to France, and the regency now fell to Bruce's grandson and the son of Walter Stewart, the seventeen-year-old Robert Stewart. Stewart took command, and with the help of the French, recaptured Perth. By 1340, Scotland was clear of the English north of the River Forth. The next year, David II returned from France and took control of the country from Stewart.

The English were distracted by a war with France, but in 1346, the King of France asked his ally for a diversion, and David II responded by leading an army into England. He was beaten at Neville's Cross and taken prisoner, where he remained at the court of Edward III for the next twelve years. Robert Stewart was once again regent.

In 1355, the French again asked for a diversion. Robert responded by recapturing Berwick while the English were defeated by William Douglas at Nesbit Muir. Edward III tried to retaliate by invading Lothian, but his troops were forced to withdraw, tired and demoralized.

Edward tried a new approach and offered to release King David II to his people for the hefty price of 100,000 marks. But David was a poor king, and Scotland was now a poorer country. David, who was on good terms with Edward, offered to surrender to England and make Edward's son his heir. The Scottish nobles were outraged. When David died in 1371, the kingdom was given not to the English but to Robert Stewart, the first Stewart king.

Chapter 4: The Stuart Dynasty

King Robert II had been a competent regent and proved to be a competent king—at first. His reign, from 1371 to 1390, was long enough and his missteps few enough that Scotland enjoyed another span of relative peace and prosperity. One of his key acts was to secure from the Scottish Parliament the hereditary passing of the crown from father to son or daughter.

The Parliament was a relatively new institution that had evolved from the king's council into a legislative body of three estates: the first estate of prelates (archbishops, bishops, abbots, etc.), the second estate of nobility (dukes, earls, viscounts, etc.), and the third estate of burgh commissioners (representatives chosen by royal burgh or cities with royal charters). The most powerful member of the first estate was the Archbishop of St. Andrews.

The history of St. Andrews Cathedral dates to the time of the Picts at a place called Cennrigmonaid. The place is believed to be an early name for the site of the Archdiocese of St. Andrews, named after the Apostle Andrew. His relics were said to have been brought to Fife, Scotland by St. Rule from Constantinople sometime in the sixth century. The relics include some of the bones of St. Andrew. According to legend, in 832 CE, the outnumbered Pictish King Óengus mac Fergusa in a battle against the Angles, vowed to make St. Andrew the patron saint of Scotland if he won. On the morning of the battle, clouds formed an X shape in the otherwise blue sky, a symbol associated with St. Andrew. Upon his victory, the king followed through with his promise. This legend is the basis for the flag of Scotland.

The flag of Scotland, a white saltire set against a celestial blue background.
https://commons.wikimedia.org/wiki/File:Flag_of_Scotland.svg

Robert II tried to place his sons into powerful seats with titles and lands. Still, much was out of his control. The powerful families of the Scottish Douglases and Northumberland Percys were at war, culminating in the Battle of Chevy Chase, famously made into an English ballad. This may have been the same battle or related to the Battle of Otterburn in 1388.

In 1390, Robert II died, and his son, Robert III, took his place on the throne. Robert III was believed to have been infirm, suffering from the results of a horse-kicking injury when he was young. He leaned heavily on his younger brother, Robert Stewart, the Duke of Albany. The government stayed in the hands of the duke, who allowed his friend, the Earl of Douglas, to continue raids into England.

Robert III's son, David Stewart, Duke of Rothesay, disappeared, died, or was killed (some suspected by order of the Duke of Albany), so the heir apparent became Robert III's young son James. Robert III had James sent to France to protect him, but the prince was captured by English pirates and became a hostage of Henry IV of England. The shock of this led to Robert III's death. While James remained in England, the Duke of Albany retained control of the government. This led to many noble families expanding their territories, consolidating power, and assembling large private armies.

None of the great Lowland families were as powerful as the Douglases, whose power rivaled the Crown. The founder of the family, James Douglas, had been a captain of Robert Bruce. His successors were made Lord Warden of the Marches and Lord of Galloway. They then became earls, and through clever marriages, increased the extent of their family connections and possessions to include Galloway, Douglasdale, Annandale, Clydesdale, Lothian, Stirling, and Morayshire. At the beginning of the Stuart dynasty, the fourth Earl of Douglas could muster an army of at least a thousand men.

In the northwest, the self-styled "Kings of the Isles," the MacDonald lords, ruled as autonomous leaders. The lords of Lorne, Argyll, and the Macleans thought of themselves as equals to the Scottish king, not subjects. Over time, the king of the Isles had become allied with the king of England. Eventually, there was a brief power struggle, but the (regent) Duke of Albany was victorious and allied with Henry IV of England.

In 1411, the University of St. Andrews was founded, followed closely by the founding of universities in Glasgow and Aberdeen. This was just the beginning of Scotland's strong tradition of learning.

Two years later, Henry IV died and was succeeded by Henry V, who attacked France and signed the Treaty of Troyes in 1420. This gave him almost half of France and the rest upon the death of the French king. However, the Dauphin, Charles, did not surrender and called upon Scotland to aid him in repelling the English. The Duke of Albany was dead, but his son, John Stewart, Earl of Buchan, brought several Scottish troops who helped turn the tide of the war. Henry V was killed in action, cursing the Scots as he died.

The new regent of Scotland was Murdoch Stewart, the former Duke of Albany's son who had inherited the title. However, James I, who was now twenty-nine and still in England, saw his path clear to claim his throne. In 1424, he returned to his kingdom, sweeping Murdoch aside. However, he did not become the puppet king that England's high council had hoped for. His reign was filled with conflict as the nobles chafed under his more direct rule. He limited the power of the church and commanded that clerics offer prayers to the king and his family.

Walter Stewart, the Earl of Atholl (son of Robert II), had urged the release of James I from England, but for various reasons, had grown to hate the king. Walter's son, David, had been taken as a hostage to England in James' place and had died there. Also, Walter was concerned that the king had designs on his many holdings and titles. He thus conspired with others who opposed the king, including his grandson, Robert Stewart, the king's chamberlain. They organized an assassination plot and carried it out on February 20, 1437. Though the king was aware of the plot as it was happening and hid from his attackers, he was found and murdered.

However, the assassins had failed to kill the queen and the six-year-old prince, who was now King James II. Walter might have been successful if he had captured the young prince, but the new king was too well protected. Robert Stewart was captured and confessed to his role in the plot. Walter was also quickly captured, along with another main conspirator, Sir Robert Graham. All three were executed. The young King James II was crowned not at Scone but at Holyrood Abbey. Archibald Douglas, 5th Earl of Douglas, became the regent. The king was put into the care of Alexander Livingston of Callendar, keeper of Stirling Castle. The king's mother, Queen Joan, soon married Sir John Stewart, the Black Knight of Lorne.

Archibald Douglas died in 1439, and the 6th Earl of Douglas was William Douglas, Archibald's son. William was invited to the Castle of Edinburgh, where he dined with the ten-year-old king. However, at the end of the dinner, a black bull's head was brought out and set before Douglas. He was soon hurried off and executed. It was known as the "Black Dinner" and was a low point in James' reign, though the young king had nothing to do with the conspiracy that was perpetrated by Sir Alexander Livingston, Lord Chancellor William Crichton, and James Douglas.

When James reached adulthood in 1449, he allied with the Douglas family to remove the Livingstons from the government for their complicity in the murder of William Douglas. However, power struggles between the king and the Douglases led to the murder of another William Douglas—the 8th Earl of Douglas—by the king's own hands. A civil war broke out, which ended with the Crown annexing much of the Douglas lands. The result was that the king no longer faced challenges to his authority from the noble ranks.

King James II was popular and known for mixing with common folk throughout his kingdom. In 1460, while laying siege to Roxburgh Castle, a cannon exploded and killed the king. This left the kingdom to his eight-year-old son, the new King James III. The king's mother, Queen

Mary of Guelders, became regent. Mary was an astute ruler but died in 1463. The king was captured by the Boyd family and forced to give them power which they abused.

James III began his personal rule in 1469, and the Boyds and their allies were declared traitors. Some went into exile, while others were captured and executed. By 1476, James had accomplished much in his reign. The Orkney and Shetland islands were officially brought under Scottish dominion, the Boyds had been dealt with, the Archbishop of St. Andrews had been bent to his will, he had concluded a successful treaty with England, and the Lord of the Isles had been greatly reduced in power. He was the undisputed ruler of a kingdom that stretched from the Northern Isles to Berwick-upon-Tweed.

However, many of his actions had made him unpopular. He had angered many nobles by favoring men of low birth and raising them to positions of power. In 1480, the truce with England had broken down following Scottish raids into English territory. In the resulting war, Richard, Duke of Gloucester (the future English King Richard III) launched a full-scale invasion across the Scottish border. However, the English were unsuccessful and retreated to their kingdom. Then, a revolt erupted within Scotland, led by the earls of Angus and Argyll. James III was killed in battle in 1488.

His son and heir was King James IV. The reign of James IV was remarkable, not just because the king was remarkable but because it was a time of peace and prosperity that Scotland had never seen. During his twenty-five years on the throne, James proved to be one of the ablest and most popular of the Stuart kings. He was well-read and excelled at languages, including Gaelic, which was no longer spoken in the Lowlands. He was charming, fun-loving, pious, and forceful. The Scottish people loved him for his open-handedness, friendliness, and his many mistresses and illegitimate children. (This was before the strict ethics of Calvinism had reached Scottish shores.) Literature flourished during his reign, including the epic poem by Blind Harry, *The Wallace*, and William Dunbar's *Thrissil and the Rois* (Thistle and the Rose) Great churches were built. Merchants' homes went from being made of wood to being made of stone. Many castles no longer looked like fortresses but began to look like palaces.

Of course, this was only true in the Lowlands. In the Highlands, life went on much as it had for many centuries. Highlanders were not very interested in the affairs of the king or the pronouncements of Parliament. The Gaelic word *clann* means children, and the chief of the Highland clan was a father, figuratively and sometimes literally, to all the members. He was he the ruler, judge, and protector. He held over them the power of life or death. When he summoned the clansmen to war, they answered at a moment's notice. The clans had their land, their cattle, and each other, and they protected it all with fervor. As the Spanish ambassador observed, "The Scots are not industrious and the people are poor. They spend all their time in wars, and when there is no war they fight one another."[1]

The lords of the Highlands were a rule unto themselves, and their lands were like small kingdoms that were often at odds with each other thanks to feuds and the ever-present need for retribution. They were the MacDonalds and MacLeods of the Western Isles, the northern Mackays, the Mackenzies just south of them, and the great clan of the Campbells at the southern edge of the Highland Line.

James did something no other Stuart king had done: he traveled into the Highlands with a strong, armed escort. He came as a friend, but his entreaties were largely ignored. After all, many of the Highlanders could trace their ancestry back to great kings who were much more admirable than the Anglicized Stuarts. As an old Maclean saying went, "Though poor, I am noble. Thank God that I am a Maclean."[2] James returned, still largely ignored by the Highlanders, and tried a different approach of force. This did not go over any better and led to a flare-up of warfare all along the Highlands. Eventually, James simply settled for placing strong posts in the Highlands and increasing the number of sheriffs and sheriff's courts.

James also greatly increased the power of the Scottish Navy. The most famous addition to the Scottish Navy was the ship *Michael*, or as it was commonly called, *Great Michael*. The ship was too large to be built at any existing Scottish dockyard, so a new dockyard was built at Newhaven. When she was launched in 1511, she was the largest ship afloat, displacing 1,000 tons and featuring twenty-seven large guns. A year later, the English King Henry VIII, not wanting to be outdone, launched the *Henry Grace à Dieu*, which was even larger.

---

[1] Maclean, Fitzroy, and Magnus Linklater. *Scotland: a concise history*. Thames & Hudson, 2000.
[2] Maclean, Fitzroy, and Magnus Linklater. *Scotland: a concise history*. Thames & Hudson, 2000.

Henry VIII was not just the king of England but also James' brother-in-law. In 1501, the twenty-eight-year-old James had married Henry's sister, Margaret Tudor, who was just twelve years old. The couple would eventually have six children. Two are nameless, and it is assumed they died in infancy. The eldest was James, born in 1507, but he died at one year of age. Next was Arthur, who died at ten months. Then came another James, Duke of Rothesay, born in 1512 and heir apparent. King James also had at least five illegitimate children by four different mothers who were all of noble origins.

James had signed a peace treaty with Henry VIII, but circumstances worked against this peace. England was, once again, at war with France. Scotland and France had enjoyed a long and beneficial alliance, often called the Auld (Old) Alliance, which had derived from their common enemy—the English.

In 1511, the pope created a Holy League against France consisting of the papacy, Spain, Venice, and the Holy Roman Empire. England joined the league, and France, seemingly without an ally, called upon Scotland. James answered the call, and in 1513, he led 40,000 men and a large amount of artillery into England. The English and Scottish forces met in the Battle of Flodden. Led by the Earl of Surrey, the English stopped the advance with a force of 26,000, while the Scottish forces had already diminished to 34,000 due to sickness and desertion. Despite having superior numbers and more modern artillery, the Scottish were defeated, and King James IV was killed in battle. A large number of the highest-ranking nobles in Scotland had also been killed, depleting the country of leadership.

The new king, James V, was barely old enough to walk. His mother, Queen Margaret Tudor, was the sister of the very man who had ordered the death of James IV and had refused to bury him. Henry VIII did this because James IV had been excommunicated by the pope for breaking the treaty with England and staying true to the Auld Alliance. However, after a year or two, things seemed to work themselves out. Henry VIII had not invaded. Queen Margaret had remarried a Scotsman and thus given up her regency. The Duke of Albany, descended from James III and newly arrived from France, was now regent, and the Holy League against France had fallen apart and saved Scotland's old ally.

After being held almost as a captive by the Douglas family, James escaped and began his reign in 1528 at the age of sixteen. He attempted to bring peace and order to the Lowlands and Borderlands and sought to appease the Highlands with varied success. James V married Marie de Guise-Lorraine, a French noblewoman.

In 1534, Henry VIII broke with Rome and created the Church of England. He wanted to impose Protestantism on Scotland as well and invaded in 1542. James retaliated by invading England, but the invasion was half-hearted, and James was soon at odds with his nobles. The king fell ill and was on his deathbed when he received word that his wife had just given birth to a daughter. The king died, and the infant girl, christened Mary, became Mary, Queen of Scots.

Chapter 5: The Reformation and the Rise of Presbyterianism

The Celtic and Pictish gods were long gone and Scotland had been completely Catholic since the beginnings of the kingdom. There had been the Celtic Catholicism of St. Columba, but Roman Catholicism had eventually overcome all. It was not just the dominant but the only religion from the Western Isles to the remaining stones of Hadrian's Wall and the screaming winds of the Orkneys. Yet, in the sixteenth century, something was sweeping across Europe and was now knocking at Scotland's door: the Protestant Reformation.

Martin Luther's *Ninety-five Theses* had been nailed to a church door in 1517. The Swiss theologian, Ulrich Zwingli, had preached on the need to reform the Catholic Church. The French theologian, John Calvin, had published his seminal work *Institutes of the Christian Religion* in 1536. As previously mentioned, Henry VIII embraced the Reformation and Protestantism in his break with the papacy, though not for primarily religious reasons. However, in Scotland in the early 1500s, Roman Catholicism was the only acceptable religious ideology.

There were certainly problems in the Catholic Church in Scotland. Most priests were poor, but there were some glaring exceptions. Parson Adam Colquhoun lived with his mistress, Mary Boyd and their two sons in a Glasgow mansion filled with gold, silver, silk, damask, gilded furniture, feather beds, and a parrot in a cage. The Bishop of Moray provided for all nine of his children from Church funds. According to reports from a cardinal, Scottish nuns were often found surrounded by their children and gave their daughters away with rich dowries taken from church revenues. Fewer people were attending mass, and many churches had fallen into disrepair.

Then, English translations of the Bible began to be smuggled into Scotland. For the first time, Scots could read the "Good Book" themselves. A young nobleman named Patrick Hamilton had come back from the continent a firm Protestant. In 1528, when Archbishop James Beaton arrested him and ordered him to recant, Hamilton refused. The young noble was burned at the stake, slowly, and it was a story of bravery recounted around the kingdom. Still, Protestantism was kept secret in Scotland for many years.

Then, in 1543, a party went to London to consider a treaty in which the English Prince Edward (son of Henry VIII) might marry the infant Mary, Queen of Scots. Accompanying this party was a Scottish scholar named George Wishart, who had earlier fled the country while being investigated for heresy. Wishart soon began to travel as an itinerant preacher, denouncing the errors of the papacy and the corruption of the Church. Along the way, he picked up a disciple by the name of John Knox. In 1546, Wishart was arrested by the orders of Bishop Beaton and then hanged.

John Knox, born near Haddington around 1513, was a firebrand and would have died alongside Wishart if his mentor had not ordered him to fall back. He had been a tutor to two sons of Hugh Douglas and one son of John Cockburn, both Scottish nobles who were reformation-minded, and he returned to this post when Wishart was captured.

Not long after Wishart's execution, Bishop Beaton was murdered by a group in retaliation for Wishart's death. A standoff of sorts then occurred as Reformers held the Castle of St. Andrew's against Catholic forces. Knox took his charges to the relative safety of the castle and was there encouraged to preach. He proved to be an excellent orator and spokesperson for the Reformist movement. The Queen Mother, Mary of Guise, who was regent, requested aid in the situation from her relations in France. Knox soon found himself captured and pressed into rowing in French galleys. After nineteen months in the galley prison, Knox was released and spent five years in England, where he was active in the Reformation.

After spending time in Geneva and Frankfurt, Knox finally returned to Scotland in 1547. He found the country greatly changed. Much of the nobility of Scotland had embraced the Reformation, and he was welcomed in many places and able to preach freely. Still, the bishops of Scotland were intimidated by his presence and called him to trial. When he arrived, he was accompanied by such a great multitude of influential and important persons that the trial was called off.

After a three-year return to Geneva, Knox once again returned to his home in 1559. He was quickly declared an outlaw by the queen regent. As Knox traveled, he preached sermons against the Catholic Church and the Catholic monarch. During many of these sermons, the crowds turned into mobs that ransacked churches and friaries.

Then in 1560, Mary of Guise died amidst an escalating war between Catholic Scots and the French against Protestant Scots and the English. This was ended by the Treaty of Edinburgh. The same year, Knox and five other Protestant ministers convened to write the Scots Confession. Knox and others also began drafting the *Book of Discipline.* These texts created the cornerstones for a new Protestant faith in Scotland known as the Reform Church but often called the Kirk (a Gaelic name meaning "church"). It would eventually be known as the Church of Scotland, or more generally, the Presbyterian Church.

Meanwhile, in 1548, the young Mary, Queen of Scots, had been sent to France, where she was expected to someday wed the Dauphin. The year before, Henry VIII had died, leaving his sickly son Edward as the new king. In 1553, King Edward VI of England died, and his sister, the very Catholic Queen Mary Tudor, took the English throne. Her reign of less than five years was tumultuous, to say the least, and earned her the immortal nickname "Bloody Mary." She died in 1558, the same year that Mary, Queen of Scots, was wed to the Dauphin of France in the Cathedral of Notre Dame in Paris.

It seemed highly likely that France and Scotland would combine into one nation—if not for the fact that France was still Catholic and Scotland was not. It was announced that the crown of England now rested on the head of the young and Protestant Queen Elizabeth I. In 1559, Mary, Queen of Scots' husband, François, succeeded to the throne of France. France soon claimed ownership of England as well because Elizabeth, being Protestant, had no right to the throne while the new French Queen Mary, granddaughter of Henry VII, could claim it. Queen Elizabeth understood the difficult situation she was in and made overtures to the Scottish Protestants—even though Knox was very vocal about his dislike of women rulers.

With Mary of Guise's death in 1560, the Scottish Protestants had won by numbers alone. The country had become Protestant even if the monarchy had not. France withdrew her claims, and the Auld Alliance came to an end. It was the first step in the union with England, and it was not the queens or kings who had made the decision but the common people.

The Kirk was a surprisingly democratic institution for the times. In a Europe that was on the verge of absolute monarchy, the Kirk at least required that ministers be voted upon by the congregation. The congregation also elected the elders, or presbyters (hence the name Presbyterian), and organized care for the poor and sick in their parish. The Kirk also became ingrained in the laws of Scotland. There were very strict rules regarding the Sabbath. For example, a person could be arrested for plucking a chicken on Sunday. There was no dancing, pipe playing, gambling, card playing, or theater acts. One of the most radical ideas of the Kirk was that, while power was given by God, it was not given to monarchs, nobles, or clergy but to the people.

Knox was assisted in much of what he did by George Buchanan, who had studied with John Calvin and Ignatius Loyola, founder of the Jesuits. Buchanan was not just a theologian but a political philosopher, and in his writings, he claimed that political authority was derived from the people. Buchanan wrote this a hundred years before similar ideas were expressed by John Locke, who was a great influence on the Founding Fathers of the United States.

At the end of 1560, after her mother had died and the Treaty of Edinburgh had been signed, Mary, Queen of Scots, was dealt another blow when her husband, the king of France, died as well. The throne of France passed to her young brother-in-law, Charles IX, and Mary returned to Scotland a Catholic monarch in a Protestant nation.

While the Protestants of Scotland welcomed her home with suspicion, the remaining Catholics found their hopes of restoring the Catholic faith in Scotland dashed. John Knox preached against her for hearing mass, dancing, and dressing too elaborately. Mary summoned Knox before her five times, but she was unsuccessful in convincing him to stop speaking out against her. On one occasion, she burst into tears, which clearly moved the minister, but he admitted he would rather endure her tears than betray his commonwealth. Mary attempted to charge him with treason in 1563, but the Privy Council, composed of Catholics and Protestants, dropped the charges against him. In July 1565, Mary married her half-first cousin Henry Stuart, Lord Darnley, in a Catholic ceremony at Holyrood Palace.

Mary was at first in love with Lord Darnley, who is usually described as lackluster, arrogant, and unintelligent, but soon became aware of his lesser qualities. She refused to grant him the Crown Matrimonial, which would make him her successor if she died. Still, Mary became pregnant with her first and only child. Six months into her pregnancy, Lord Darnley became increasingly jealous of her Italian secretary, David Rizzio. In March 1566, Lord Darnley, along with Protestant confederates, stabbed Rizzio fifty-six times, killing him. All the accounts agree that the murder took place in front of the pregnant queen. According to some, Rizzio was the true father of Mary's child, and Darnley's action had been designed to force Mary to give him the Crown Matrimonial. Still, Mary did not acquiesce. On June 19, Mary gave birth to a son named James, the heir to the throne.

Mary and Lord Darnley's marriage continued to struggle. Lord Darnley alienated those who would have support him. He came down with a case of smallpox (though some suggested syphilis), and Mary took him to the Old Provost's lodging at Kirk o' Field, which was a short walk from Holyrood. On the night of February 9, 1567, Mary was attending the wedding of one of her favorite servants while Darnley remained in Kirk o' Field. Around 2 a.m., two explosions rocked the foundations of Kirk o' Field, probably caused by gunpowder barrels placed under Lord Darnley's sleeping quarters. Lord Darnley's dead body and the body of his valet, William Taylor, were found outside the house along with a cloak, dagger, chair, and coat. There were no marks on Lord Darnley's body, so it is believed he was smothered to death. Still, it was clear that Lord Darnley had been murdered. Though it was never proven, James Hepburn, Earl of Bothwell and Lord High Admiral, was heavily implicated.

Eight weeks after Lord Darnley's murder, Mary married James Hepburn, Earl of Bothwell, in a Protestant ceremony. This decision turned both Catholics and Protestants against the queen.

A month later, a group of nobles known as the Confederate Lords gathered an army to rescue Mary from Lord Bothwell, responding to rumors that Lord Bothwell had kidnapped and raped the queen. At Carberry Hill, the forces of Lord Bothwell met the army of the Confederate Lords, and the queen's supporters were defeated. Lord Bothwell escaped, but the queen surrendered. Mary, only twenty-four years old, was led through the streets of Edinburgh in a short red petticoat amid much derision. On June 1567, she was forced to abdicate the throne in favor of her infant son. That son was crowned King James VI. John Knox delivered a sermon on the occasion and called for Mary's death. Mary's Protestant half-brother, James Stewart, Earl of Moray, was made regent.

Mary was held prisoner at Lochleven Castle near Kinross. She escaped with the assistance of her jailers in 1586 and raised another army but was again defeated, this time by the Earl of Moray. Finally, she crossed the English border in a fishing boat and threw herself at the mercy of England's Queen Elizabeth I. Mary apparently expected Elizabeth to help restore her to the throne of Scotland, but Elizabeth was wary. For one thing, Mary was Catholic while Elizabeth was aligned with the Protestants in Scotland. Secondly, Mary had a claim to the English throne through her grandmother, Margaret Tudor. Elizabeth kept her imprisoned and constantly on the move.

Young King James VI was raised primarily at Stirling Castle, where he was educated to be a member of the Scottish Presbyterian Church. The Protestant nobles of Scotland who had just fought against a Catholic monarch had no interest in repeating history. George Buchanan became the chief of the young king's tutors. He passed on to him regular beatings but also a love of reading and education. In 1570, James' regent, the Earl of Moray, was assassinated by James Hamilton, a supporter of James' mother, Mary. Queen Elizabeth saw the assassination and a corresponding revolt of Catholic nobles in northern England as a sign of Mary's danger. She was kept under close supervision by Elizabeth's chief advisor, William Cecil.

The next regent of Scotland was the Earl of Lennox, James' paternal grandfather. Lennox was killed a year later by supporters of Mary. The Earl of Mar was then made regent, but he, too, died shortly thereafter of a mysterious illness, possibly poisoning. James Douglas, Earl of Morton, became the next regent and remained in that capacity until 1579 when King James was fifteen and declared an adult able to rule on his own.

Morton was quickly executed for treason.

After an initial struggle, James consolidated power to himself. One of his chief problems was the role of the Reformed Church in Scotland. He enacted the Black Acts, which brought the Kirk partly under royal control—a decision that would have surely upset James' old tutor George Buchanan had the great thinker not died two years before. The reformist, John Knox, had also died in relative obscurity in 1572. Still, the Presbyterian ministers who followed Knox and Buchanan's *Book of Discipline* felt that the power of the monarchy came from the Kirk. While King James was certainly a Protestant, he was not a Presbyterian. Instead, he felt that the church's power was derived from God's chosen ruler, the king. In this episcopal view, the church was ruled by bishops who were appointed by the monarch—exactly what was done in the Church of England.

In 1584, Mary, Queen of Scots, had agreed to give up any pretensions to the English throne and to retire from public life if only she could be freed from her imprisonment. James at first entertained the idea but then reconsidered and signed an alliance with Elizabeth, abandoning his mother to her fate.

In 1586, Mary was implicated in the Babington Plot to assassinate Queen Elizabeth. She was put on trial for treason, and her defense was spirited. She argued that she had not been able to review the evidence or seek legal counsel and that since she had never been a subject of England, she could not be tried for treason. However, her personal letters made it clear she had approved of the assassination plot, and she was found guilty and sentenced to death. Elizabeth was hesitant to carry out the sentence as she was concerned about setting the precedent of killing a queen. She also feared King James' reaction to the death of his mother. Still, she went through with it, and Mary, Queen of Scots, was beheaded on February 8, 1587.

James made a public declaration of complaint but did nothing to jeopardize his relationship with the English queen. He knew quite well that if Elizabeth died without an heir, which she was almost certain to do, he would have the best claim to the throne of England. In 1603, Queen Elizabeth died, and James was proclaimed king of England later the same day. While this meant that Scotland and England shared a monarch, it did not mean they were united in any other way. They had separate parliaments, laws, courts, and churches, though they did share a similar language. (The Scottish version of English, called "Scots," had been the standard language of the country for centuries. Gaelic was only spoken in a few corners of the kingdom.)

While the two kingdoms were not truly united, James styled himself "King of Great Britain" and forced the Scottish Parliament to use the title, which was used in proclamations and coinage. James moved his court to London and only returned to Scotland once in his long reign.

The change in Scotland was profound. The Scottish people developed an inferiority complex regarding their southern neighbors. No longer were they twin kingdoms on the same island; now England was clearly the favorite sibling. The king preferred England, and Scotland was constantly fending off the invasion of English episcopalian religion, English culture, and English dominance. Scottish nobles flocked to London to work their way into royal affairs. The stereotype of the tight-fisted Scot vying for his share was born.

In 1606, the leader of the Kirk and theological heir of John Knox, Andrew Melville, was imprisoned in the Tower of London by order of the king after speaking out against the popish character of an Anglican service. He was held in the tower for four years. When he was finally freed, he was forced into exile in France, where he remained for the rest of his life.

James introduced more episcopalian elements to the Kirk, and when he died in 1625, the Church of Scotland had a complete assortment of bishops and archbishops. James' son, Charles I, became king of Scotland and England and continued to force episcopalian services and rituals into Scotland. He believed, as his father had, that Presbyterianism was incompatible with the monarchy. The introduction of Charles' *Scottish Prayer Book* in 1637 led to rioting that spread across the kingdom. The rioting, in turn, led to the First Bishops' War in 1639, which only resulted in a few skirmishes, followed by the Second Bishops' War in 1640. The result was a defeat for Charles and a somewhat insignificant truce between him and the Scottish nobles.

Then Charles was forced to deal with a rebellion in Ireland in 1641. Finally, the English Civil War erupted, setting the king against the English Parliament. Charles was eventually captured and, in a surprise move, signed a secret treaty with a faction of Scots. They would invade England and restore the king to his throne on the agreement that Presbyterianism would be impressed on England for three years. The

Scots invaded but were defeated by the New Model Army under the command of Oliver Cromwell. Charles was tried, found guilty of treason, and beheaded on January 30, 1649.

While England became a republic, the Scottish Covenanter Parliament agreed to crown Charles' son, Charles II, as the King of Scotland—but only if he agreed to make Presbyterianism the state religion. In 1651, Charles II agreed to the Covenanter Parliament's demands and was crowned king. His abandonment of episcopalian religion was unpopular in England and led to a war in which Cromwell defeated a Scottish force yet again. Charles II led an invasion force into England but (like his father) was defeated, though he managed to escape to Normandy. Cromwell then put the British Isles under military rule, which ended when Cromwell died in 1658. Charles II was invited back to England and crowned in 1661.

Once again, the king of Scotland, Ireland, and England was the same man, and England became the focal point of the monarch's attention. However, it was not just tradition but economics that played a role in England's status. The southern British kingdom now had colonies around the globe and a burgeoning global empire.

Scottish immigration to the English American colonies had begun in 1650 when Cromwell had sent defeated Scots to Maine, Massachusetts, and New Hampshire. Voluntary Scottish immigration soon followed, especially to the Carolinas and New Jersey. Yet, long before this, in 1629, the Scottish had founded the colony of Nova Scotia. However, this colony was soon abandoned and handed over to the French after the Treaty of Suza.

The most well-known and disastrous of Scotland's colonial attempts was the settlement of New Caledonia on the shore of the isthmus of Panama in 1698. It was called the Darien scheme after the colony's location—the Gulf of Darien.

The Wars of the Three Kingdoms that preceded the restoration of Charles II had been hard on Scotland, but so were the "Seven Ill Years" in the 1690s, which brought widespread crop failure and a huge loss of life. As a result of these hard times, the Scottish Parliament enacted wide-sweeping programs to improve the lives of the Scottish people. The Bank of Scotland, based on the very successful Bank of England, was formed. The Act of Settling Schools was passed, which created a school in every parish in the country. This radical legislation would have far-reaching consequences: a generation later, the Scottish people were widely regarded as the most well-read and educated people in Western Europe.

Parliament also created the Company of Scotland, which it hoped to rival the great colonial companies of Africa, Asia, and the West Indies. However, the East India Company saw this as a direct threat. As a result, the Company of Scotland found it all but impossible to raise funds from English or Dutch investors. The new king, William II (and III of England), gave only mild support to the cause because he did not want to upset the Spanish, who claimed all of Panama for themselves. Consequently, the Scottish people, both noble and common, provided all the funds for the expedition, which amounted to £400,000 sterling— roughly one-fifth of all the wealth in the country.

Five ships sailed from Leith in July 1698 and landed near the mouth of the Darien River in November. The expedition consisted of 1,200 people, many of them former soldiers. They built a fort and a watchtower and then constructed a group of huts they called "New Edinburgh." Growing crops proved difficult, the natives were unwilling to trade, and disease began to run rampant through the colony. The few trading vessels that stopped were not interested in the trinkets the Scots had brought with them. To avoid angering the Spanish, King William instructed the English and Dutch not to provide supplies to the Scots.

After just eight months, the colony was abandoned. Only 300 of the original 1,200 survived, and two ships limped into New York harbor. The only colonists who made it home were considered a disgrace and disowned by their families. However, the fate of the colony did not reach Scotland in time to stop another 1,000 brave souls headed to Panama. This group rebuilt and took the offensive against the Spanish, but this only led to the Spanish besieging the settlers' fort until they surrendered. It was the last attempt at a Scottish colony.

Then in 1702, William II died and was succeeded by his sister-in-law, Anne. Queen Anne had been the sister of William's wife, Queen Mary, and the daughter of the unpopular James II. In her first speech to Parliament, trying to distance herself from her Dutch brother-in-law, she said, "As I know my heart to be entirely English, I can very sincerely assure you there is not anything you can expect or desire from me which

I shall not be ready to do for the happiness and prosperity of England."[3] This must have come as a bitter pill to her Scottish subjects. Yet, Scotland was in no state to argue. The Darien scheme had wrecked the economy, and famine and cold had decimated the population. It was five years later that Queen Anne proposed a union between the two kingdoms of Britain.

---

[3] Maclean, Fitzroy, and Magnus Linklater. *Scotland: a concise history.* Thames & Hudson, 2000.

Chapter 6: Union with England— The 1707 Act of Union and Its Consequences

King William III of England, also known as William of Orange.
https://commons.wikimedia.org/wiki/File:King_William_III_of_England,_(1650-1702).jpg

It was a long and winding road that led to the 1707 Act of Union that dissolved the Scottish and English governments to create a new British government. Of course, the relationship between the two countries had long been fraught with tension and occasionally escalated to outright bloodshed, as a review of these events will show.

As we mentioned, the ascendancy of the Scottish King James VI to the throne of England as James I did not suddenly unite the kingdoms but instead did quite the reverse. The Scots felt ignored at best and oppressed at worst. James did all he could to turn the Scots into Englishmen. James' son, Charles, had been born in Scotland but left for England when he was three in 1603. He did not return until 1633 after he had been king for eight years. He had no understanding of Scotland and was a devout episcopalian with a strong dislike of democratic assemblies. In 1629, he demanded that the religious practices of Scotland should conform to the Church of England. When he finally bothered to come to Scotland to be crowned, it was done with full Anglican rites.

By 1638, Charles had only made matters worse. Representatives from the nobles, gentry, burghs, and clergy met to sign a document called the National Covenant, which opposed Charles' demands but did not call for revolution. Soon, the document was copied and distributed throughout the country, and many more signed. From this came the cascading events that led to the Bishops' Wars and eventually the English Civil War.

The Scots were in a good position during the war. The Covenanters (those who followed the National Covenant) signed the Solemn League and Covenant with the English Parliament to do just the thing they hated Charles for—namely, forcing their religion onto the English. But this was undone by another Scot and a former Covenanter, James Graham the 1st Marquess of Montrose (known as the Great Montrose), who rose in support of King Charles. With an army of Irish and Highlanders, he began crushing larger armies and sacking important cities throughout Scotland. Montrose was eventually defeated, but his actions undermined the Covenanters' power, which had shifted to Oliver Cromwell and his army. Cromwell had no interest in dealing with the Covenanters or seeing Presbyterianism in England.

The Scots then handed over Charles but almost instantly questioned this decision. They began plotting with the imprisoned king to bring him back to the throne and impose Presbyterianism on England. This, of course, failed to happen, and when the news reached Scotland that Charles had been executed, the universal response was shock. No matter how much the Covenanters opposed Charles, they never imagined he might be killed.

The Great Montrose's chief opponent and the primary power among the Covenanters, Archibald Campbell, the 1st Marquess of Argyll, immediately contacted Charles I's son, also Charles, and proclaimed him king in Edinburgh. After initial failures and the eventual death of Cromwell, Charles II was on the throne of England and administered Scotland, like his father and grandfather before him, through a Privy Council. Despite the support of people like Argyll, Charles II soon undid all the measures enacted by the Covenanters. Many openly defied him, and violent outbursts ensued.

Charles II died in 1685 and was succeeded by his brother James VII and II, the Duke of York, who had been born in the Church of England but converted to Catholicism while in France. Archibald Campbell organized a rebellion against the new king. This was encouraged by James' Dutch son-in-law, William of Orange. However, the rebellion was a failure, and Campbell was executed.

James' policies were increasingly unpopular. When his second (Catholic) wife gave birth to a son, thus confirming the likelihood of a new Catholic dynasty in both countries, a group of nobles invited William of Orange and his wife, Mary the daughter of James, to come to Britain with an army. In 1689, William and Mary landed in England. James soon fled, and the Protestant couple were crowned king and queen. The Glorious Revolution was complete.

There were some, especially in the Highlands, who remained true to King James VII. These formed the first group to be called Jacobites. William sent an army to defeat a Jacobite army in Perthshire, but his army, led by General James Mackay, was annihilated. However, the Highlanders soon faded back into their homes in the mountains and glens.

William decided to set an example and demanded an oath of fealty from the clan heads by January 1, 1692. A rebellion was avoided when the exiled James sent word that the Highlanders should comply. Only two did not meet the deadline. One was the leader of the powerful MacDonells of Glengarry, and the other was MacIain, the chieftain of a minor sept (branch) of Clan Donald, the MacDonalds of Glencoe. MacIain arrived to take the oath on January 6, unable to make the journey to the proposed location due to inclement weather. The MacDonell leader was forgiven, but MacIain became William's example.

A group of Robert Campbell's troops arrived as guests in Glencoe. They spent weeks drinking and playing cards until they received the orders to put the entire sept to the sword. On February 13, early in the morning, the troops systematically slaughtered the MacDonalds as they slept and burned their cottages to the ground. William succeeded in putting a temporary halt to Jacobinism in the Highlands, but Scotland grew to distrust their new monarch.

It was not until the Darien scheme (detailed in the last chapter) that many Scots began to see the only way of saving their country from ruin was through union with England. In 1702, Queen Anne (William's sister-in-law) came to the throne, but she had no heir. The English were concerned about another Stuart restoration as James VII and II's son, James Edward, was alive and still a Roman Catholic. So, the English signed the 1701 Act, establishing that the throne would pass through Sophia, the Electress of Hanover, a German princess and the granddaughter of James VI and I.

However, the English were also concerned that the Stuarts might come through the "back door," meaning the throne of Scotland. The Scots, aware of the situation, passed the Act of Security. This said the successor to the Scottish throne would be a Protestant descendant from the House of Stuart—but not the same monarch as in England unless Scotland was given equal trading rights and freedom of government and religion. The English were incensed by this bold move, and tensions rose. The queen could not afford a war with Scotland since she was already at war with France. In 1705, she sent the young Duke of Argyll, the Lord High Commissioner, to persuade the Scottish Parliament to authorize negotiations for a Treaty of Union.

So on October 3, 1707, the Scottish Parliament met in Edinburgh to vote on the Treaty of Union. The treaty had been negotiated by two teams of commissioners, one Scottish and one English, but there was little to negotiate as both parties were handpicked by Queen Anne and devised the treaty exactly according to her specifications.

Quite simply, the Crown wanted the incorporation of Scotland into England. The treaty created the Kingdom of Great Britain, governed by one monarch and one Parliament. The seat of government would be in London. The Scottish Privy Council would lose all its power, while England assumed control over taxes, customs, and excise duties for both nations as well as over military and foreign affairs. The Scottish Parliament would dissolve, and in its place, the Scottish would have forty-five seats out of 558 in the new British Parliament. Only sixteen Scottish nobles would be allowed into the House of Peers.

The appointed head of the pro-union forces in Parliament was James Douglas, Marquis of Queensbury. London had given him 20,000 pounds to buy the votes if needed. Ultimately, he didn't need the whole amount and pocketed 12,000 pounds for his troubles. The Scottish nobility had fallen on hard times, and the promise of access to the English trade routes that encircled the globe was something they couldn't reject on any grounds.

The spokesperson for the motley collection of anti-unionists was one of the founders of the Darien scheme, Andrew Fletcher of Saltoun. Fletcher was an enigmatic figure. In 1685, he had joined the Earl of Argyll in opposing James VII and II's succession but was sent abroad for murdering Argyll's chief guide. In exile, Fletcher became friends with William of Orange but turned against him after the Glorious Revolution, realizing that William wasn't going to set Scotland free. For all his supposed love of freedom, Fletcher once proposed turning the entirety of the Scottish peasantry into slaves.

In the Parliament's consideration of the Treaty of Union, there were twenty-five articles to consider separately. First and foremost was the ability of Scottish merchants to enter English overseas markets. The pro-union side argued that, while it sounded like Scotland was giving up political autonomy, this was an illusion. London had been administering Scottish affairs for over a century. If the Parliament dissolved, the only people who'd notice were the members themselves.

Still, the anti-union party, or at least a portion of it, was more concerned with the future of Scotland's religion. The treaty said nothing about the Kirk, and Presbyterian ministers widely opposed the treaty for fear that England would use its power to dismantle the church. Then, at the last moment, the General Assembly of the Kirk of Scotland gave its consent to the treaty. The assembly had been won over by the efforts of

William Carstares, principal of the University of Edinburgh and moderator of the General Assembly.

Finally, on November 4, Parliament voted in favor of the first article—the creation of Great Britain. The next two articles passed, as well. Article 4, which concerned the freedom of trade, was next on the docket. This was when Fletcher rose to make his rebuttal to the chief reason pro-unionists supported the treaty. In an eloquent speech, he explained that while England might prosper from trade, Scotland never could. It was not in the nature of the Scottish to be merchants. His speech fell on deaf ears, and the article passed with 156 votes for and 19 against.

Over the next two months, Parliament made its way through the rest of the articles with little opposition. Then came Article 22, which abolished the Scottish Parliament. The debate began with John Dalrymple, 1st Earl of Stair. Dalrymple was a man without sympathy who had been largely responsible for the massacre at Glencoe. He called the people killed, including women and children, a "sept of thieves." Dalrymple explained that the limited number of seats for Scotland in the new Parliament made absolute sense. The English, collectively, would be paying thirty-five times more in taxes than the Scots. So, their numbers in Parliament should reflect that. Really, Dalrymple argued, Scotland was getting the better of the deal at ten-to-one representation.

Article 22 passed by forty votes. Dalrymple left the chambers, exhausted, and returned to his Edinburgh lodgings, where he went to sleep and never woke up. He was declared a martyr to the cause of union.

Not long after, Parliament voted in favor of the rest of the articles and then on the whole treaty. The Kingdom of Scotland thus ceased to exist. "Now there's an end to an old song," remarked Lord Seafield.[1] Due to the angry mob in Edinburgh that opposed the treaty, the members had to sign the final documents secretly and then promptly flee to London.

Part of the treaty involved compensation for investors who had lost so much in the Darien scheme. Many were rewarded for their pro-union votes—but perhaps not as much as they hoped. The Marquis of Queensberry benefited the most, of course, and was awarded an earldom by the queen and a year stipend.

---

[1] Maclean, Fitzroy, and Magnus Linklater. *Scotland: a concise history.* Thames & Hudson, 2000.

In the short term, it seemed that those opposed to the treaty were right. The English made it clear that Scotland was subservient to England, and despite promises otherwise, Presbyterians were not secure. Scotland was once again being primed for revolution.

Chapter 7: Jacobite Risings

The general unrest in Scotland over the union encouraged the Jacobites, who hoped for the return of James Francis Edward (James VII and II's son) and the Stuart dynasty, to push toward their goal. When Queen Anne fell ill in 1714, a Jacobite coup seemed possible. When Anne subsequently died, Parliament acted quickly and proclaimed her German cousin, son of the Electress Sophia, King George I of the House of Hanover. The new monarch was generally disagreeable to his subjects. He was unattractive physically and personally to the British people, and (early in his reign, at least) he did not even speak English. Though he was Protestant, he was neither Anglican nor Presbyterian but Lutheran.

Two political factions grew during this time. Whigs typically supported King George and the nobility, while Tories drew support from the landed gentry. Many opposed George in favor of the Catholic James Francis Edward Stuart.

John Erskine, the 6th Earl of Mar, had originally favored the union even though he would be forced to surrender his position as the Secretary of State of Scotland. He had hoped he could secure a lucrative position in George's government, but the king completely ignored him. Lord Mar left London in haste. In 1715, he called on his friends and dependents to join him in a traditional stag hunt. After the hunt, while drinking honeyed whiskey, Lord Mar told those gathered that he now regretted his support for the "cursed union" and pledged to undo it and return Scotland to her ancient liberties.

According to some sources, Lord Mar, known as "Bobbing John" to his contemporaries due to his frequent changes in loyalty, had received a letter from James Edward directing him to take this action. Other sources claim James was ignorant of the plot until after Mar had proclaimed him king.

When Lord Mar raised the Scottish standard at Castletown in Braemar, the ornamental ball on top of the flagpole fell off and struck the ground. This caused a murmur among the more superstitious present, but Lord Mar took no notice. He quickly raised an army of 12,000 clansmen, who all declared for King James in a rising called "the Fifteen" for the year in which it took place, 1715.

The rising had a good start, and Lord Mar soon captured Perth. All that stood in his way to the English border was 2,000 soldiers under the command of John Campbell, 2nd Duke of Argyll. However, Lord Mar might have been an excellent politician, but he was not a military leader. He stayed in Perth for several weeks, missing the opportunity for decisive action. He sent his best commander, Mackintosh of Borlum, with 2,000 troops to meet with Jacobites on both sides of the Scottish and English border.

Old Borlum, as he was known, took it upon himself to move toward Edinburgh, but he was headed off by the experienced Duke of Argyll. After turning south and combining forces with William Gordon, 6th Viscount of Kenmure, and Thomas Forster, an English Jacobite, the army met the Duke of Argyll in the Battle of Preston. Under the command of Forster, the Jacobite army was defeated, and Forster offered his surrender. Many Jacobites were captured, and some were executed—including the Viscount of Kenmure. Both Borlum and Forster were captured but managed to escape.

Meanwhile, Simon Fraser, 11th Lord Lovat (the contested Chief of Clan Fraser), had returned to raise his clan. Fraser was known as "the Fox" and, by that time, had double dealings, death sentences, a forced marriage, and imprisonment in his past. His claim as Lord of Lovat had been in doubt when Alexander Mackenzie had married the heiress to the title and moved into the Lovat home of Beaufort Castle. Yet, Simon still commanded the allegiance of many of the Frasers who did not recognize Mackenzie's leadership.

Fraser had been imprisoned in France but was then allowed to go to London, where he was living when the 1715 uprising broke out. He asked the Crown to be allowed to go home and raise his clan. He was given permission, but knowing the history of "the Fox," the English questioned his motives. Fraser erased all doubt when he led his clan to seize Inverness Castle on behalf of King George. The Frasers that had joined Lord Mar defected, as did many of the Gordons. For his trouble, Simon was given a full pardon and restored to his position as Lord of Lovat, once again able to collect the income associated with it. Andrew Mackenzie, who had joined the Jacobite cause, was captured and thrown in jail. The Whig clans of the north soon controlled the whole region.

Lord Mar once again advanced on the Duke of Argyll, and the armies met at Sheriffmuir. Lord Mar's right routed the duke's left, while the duke's right did the same to Lord Mar's left. The Duke of Argyll suffered more losses than Lord Mar, but Lord Mar had once again failed to push his advantage, and this allowed the Duke of Argyll to retreat. The battle was indecisive, but in a wider sense, it was a great loss for the Jacobites. The Duke of Argyll still held Stirling and still blocked Lord Mar's progress to England. Lord Mar continued to wallow in Perth, losing large numbers of soldiers daily as the Highlanders again faded into their mountains and glens.

Perhaps the most startling thing to consider is that the fall of Inverness Castle at the Battle of Preston and the indecisive Battle of Sheriffmuir happened on roughly the same day— November 13, 1715. Once the news reached Lord Mar, it became apparent that the uprising had lost, and the Jacobite cause would need to be deferred. Still, Lord Mar remained in Perth.

Then, in December 1715, James Francis Edward Stuart, known to his enemies as James the Pretender, landed at Peterhead just north of Aberdeen. The cause to restore the Stuarts to the throne was already lost. He took the situation in his typical melancholy fashion. "For me it is no new thing to be unfortunate," he said to those gathered, "since my whole life from my cradle has been a constant series of misfortunes."[5] Lord Mar soon abandoned Perth. Once he reached Montrose, he and James took a ship to France. James left a message for the Jacobite Highlanders, who remained to save themselves.

The British government then set about restoring peace to Scotland. Many rebels were taken prisoner and executed. However, in 1717, the

---

[5] Maclean, Fitzroy, and Magnus Linklater. *Scotland: a concise history*. Thames & Hudson, 2000.

Indemnity Act, also called the Act of Grace and Free Pardon, freed most of the prisoners and allowed them to settle at home or overseas. However, there were exceptions, most notably the entire Clan Gregor, who were mostly known as outlaws. This included the famous Rob Roy Macgregor, who had joined the 1715 Jacobite Rising and afterward terrorized the Highlands as an outlaw who waged war on James Graham, the 1st Duke of Montrose. He was immortalized in Sir Walter Scott's novel *Rob Roy*, which deals with the time of the Fifteen. John Erskine's title, the Earl of Mar (which was made a dukedom by James the Pretender), was forfeited and remained vacant for over a century.

When James Francis Edward left Scotland, many of the Scottish people had little reason to love him; on his return to France, he was not welcome either. His patron, French King Louis XIV, had died, and France had aligned with the House of Hanover. James finally settled in the Italian walled city of Urbino and then in Rome as a guest of Pope Innocent XIII. There, he created a Stuart court in exile and lived in splendor, though he still dealt with waves of melancholy. In 1719, he married a Polish princess, and together they had two sons: Charles Edward and Henry Benedict.

Then, in 1719, the Jacobites found they had a very powerful ally in Cardinal Giulio Alberoni, a powerful statesman in the Spanish court under Philip V. Alberoni probably didn't care whether a Stuart or Hanover occupied the throne of Scotland, but he was interested in distracting England, which had joined the Quadruple Alliance against Spain.

Alberoni sent William Mackenzie, the 5th Earl of Seaforth, and George Keith, 10th Earl Marischal, who were in exile after participating in the rising of 1715, to begin a new rising in the Highlands. Accompanying them were two frigates and 300 Spanish soldiers. He would also send twenty-seven ships and 5,000 troops directly to England. The larger party was scattered by storms and never made it. In fact, there has been some speculation that Alberoni never intended for that landing to go through.

The Scottish party landed and marched to Glenshiel, where they were met by superior government forces. They were soon defeated. The Spanish surrendered, and the Scots dispersed into the hills. Earl Marischal returned to exile with James the Pretender, who made him part of his Order of the Garter. He soon found service within the government of Prussia. Seaforth would later be pardoned by George II.

The British government continued with measures to pacify the Highlands. In 1720, efforts were made to stamp out the Gaelic language, and in 1725, Highlanders were banned from carrying arms in public. Under General Wade, a program of road building began to penetrate the most important regions and connect them to Fort William, Fort Augustus, and Fort George. Several Independent Highland Companies were recruited by Whig leaders and formed a regiment called the Black Watch, which performed police duties.

In 1727, George I was succeeded by his son, George II. England's attitude toward Scotland remained much the same. Taxes became a perpetual point of contention, especially on malt (an ingredient in whiskey) and salt, which led to riots. Smuggling became common, and smugglers were popular heroes. The House of Hanover reacted with harsh punishment, which did nothing to endear them to their Scottish subjects.

England was again at war with Spain in 1739, followed the next year by war with France. The Jacobites saw an opportunity in Prince Charles Edward Stuart, a young man of energy, courage, and charisma. In January 1744, Bonnie Prince Charlie, as he would be called, left his father in Rome and headed to France. His hope of being recognized as heir to the throne of England, Scotland, and Ireland by Louis XV went unfulfilled. Even many of the Jacobites in Scotland seemed reluctant to support him.

So, after he sold some of his mother's jewelry, Prince Charles outfitted a frigate and a ship of the line and set sail for Scotland. The ship, *Elizabeth*, turned back, but the frigate, *Doutelle*, landed on the island of Eriskay in the Outer Hebrides. The nobles there refused to see Charles, and one told him to go home. "I am come home," he replied[6].

Prince Charles then went to Moidat, where Clan MacDonald of Clanranald rallied to his cause. An army of 900 was raised, and Charles' father, James, was once again proclaimed king. The prince gathered 3,000 clansmen and marched on Edinburgh, which he captured. He then defeated government forces at Prestonpans. But he lingered in Edinburgh for more than a month.

---

[6] Maclean, Fitzroy, and Magnus Linklater. *Scotland: a concise history*. Thames & Hudson, 2000.

George II recalled Dutch and English troops from Flanders, while Prince Charles hoped for support from France. The French sent supplies and money, but no troops. In November, he crossed the border and headed toward London. He hoped to be joined by English Jacobites, but this did not happen. Charles' position was advanced on by three separate armies: General Wade from the northeast, the Duke of Chamberlain through the Midlands, and another from the capital. In all, Charles was surrounded by some 30,000 troops to his roughly 5,000 clansmen.

Charles' council advised him to retreat, which he finally agreed to. He had an indecisive battle at Falkirk and then met the Duke of Cumberland's army at the Battle of Culloden. The prince's army was exhausted, hungry, and ill-prepared while Cumberland, who was the son of George II and also a prince, had an army that was well-trained, well-rested, and well-fed. Charles' army was crushed at every point. Bonnie Prince Charlie watched with tears as his hopes of a Stuart restoration were washed away in blood.

The Battle of Culloden would be called the Forty-five Rebellion or simply the Forty-Five, and it was the last serious attempt to put James Edward Stuart on the throne of Scotland or England. After the defeat at Culloden, one of Charles' generals, Lord George Murray, Duke of Atholl, organized a retreat to Ruthven Barracks to continue the fight, but Prince Charles told the army to disperse. Lord Murray left for France, hoping to return.

The Scots who had joined this last revolt felt understandably ill-used. They had risked their lives and titles on promises from exiled Scots with little to lose and Bonnie Prince Charlie's promises of English and French support that never materialized. Lord Murray, like many of the Jacobite nobles, went into exile and petitioned James Stuart in Rome, where he received a pension.

Lord Murray's younger brother, James, however, had been part of Lord Cumberland's army at Culloden. James Murray became the 2nd Duke of Atholl since both of his older brothers had joined the 1719 and 1745 Jacobite rebellions. James, unlike his brothers, was loyal to the House of Hanover, and his loyalty was rewarded. He was made Lord Privy Seal and invested with the Order of the Thistle. He gained the baronage of Strange and sovereignty of the Isle of Man. Thus, he was both a Scottish peer and an English baron. He sat in the British

Parliament with much prestige. James was succeeded as Duke of Atholl by his brother George's son, John Murray. John was married to James Murray's daughter, Charlotte (his first cousin), who inherited the rest of her father's titles.

After the Battle of Culloden, Prince Charles fled first to Gorthleck and then to Invergarry Castle. He was aware that government forces were hunting for him and fled again, always one step ahead of his pursuers. Highlanders aided him in his flight, promising not to tell anyone of his whereabouts. He then made for The Hebrides, going secretly from island to island. Flora MacDonald, a minor noble who was not known to support the Jacobite cause, helped him sail to the Isle of Skye. Charles was disguised as an Irish maid named "Betty Burke." MacDonald was arrested for her part in the ruse and was held in the Tower of London. She was eventually freed under the Act of Indemnity of 1747.

Charles returned to mainland Scotland and eventually took a ship to France. King Louis XV welcomed him warmly but was not forthcoming with any aid to the cause of the Stuart restoration. Charles soon fell out with his brother Henry, who had joined the Catholic Church as a cardinal, and his father, James. Charles later went so far as to renounce his Catholic faith to gain support from the Protestants in Scotland and England, but it did not help.

In 1766, James, the Old Pretender, died. Pope Clement XIII had recognized James as the rightful king of Scotland, England, and Ireland but did not extend this same recognition to Charles, his heir. Charles could not gather any support for his cause and, in his later years, fell into drunkenness. He referred to himself as the "Duke of Albany" and in his will passed on this title to his illegitimate daughter, Charlotte. He died of a stroke in 1788.

Three Scottish lords were beheaded after the Forty-five, but most of those involved were pardoned. The military road system was completed by the government, and more forts were added in the Highlands. The clan system was further weakened with additional political measures. The most significant was the Heritable Jurisdictions (Scotland) Act of 1746, which ended the feudal power of chiefs over clansmen. Highland dress was outlawed, though this restriction was later repealed.

The Jacobite movement did not completely end after 1745, but it ceased to be a major consideration for the government. Never again would a large army threaten to restore the Stuart dynasty by force. The

Duke of Cumberland, soon after his victory at Culloden, resigned from the military and died of a stroke in 1765.

Debate about the exact motives of the last Jacobite rebellion continues. Certainly, various people joined the cause for various reasons. Prince Charles, despite his image of being courageous and charming, was not quite the leader the Jacobites had hoped for. Many joined the cause not because they opposed the House of Hanover but because they opposed the union and hoped for a free Scottish kingdom or even republic. Scottish exiles had joined Charles because he offered the opportunity to not just win back the titles and land they had lost but to gain more in the process.

All of these were a threat to the established government in London, and many Scots declined to involve themselves in Jacobite risings. Continuous warfare had drained them in many ways, and the new unified British government was not just as good as any government they had had before. In many ways, it was better, and it continued to get better as the union progressed.

Chapter 8: The Scottish Enlightenment

Scottish philosopher David Hume.

The Scottish Enlightenment started to pick up just as the dust was settling from the Jacobite risings of 1715 and 1719. It continued through the Forty-Five and into the nineteenth century. Many of the writers, scientists, philosophers, and teachers of the Scottish Enlightenment could also be found in armed militia protecting the cities from the army of Bonnie Prince Charlie. They were all Whigs and supporters of the House of Hanover and the new British government.

The English began thinking of Scotland as a newly acquired province, but the great minds of the Enlightenment showed them that Scotland could rival and overcome them in areas where only the "gentleman" was allowed. The Scottish might have had rough accents and might have stood openmouthed before the sprawling metropolis of London, but they could also be brilliant. Their fierce tongues and wit could drive them to amazing feats of intelligence.

When the Scottish writer James Boswell met the English writer Samuel Johnson, Boswell apologized for being Scottish. and Johnson accepted that it was something many Scottish people were sorry for. Still, Johnson took Boswell under his wing because he saw something in the young man from Edinburgh; this would be revealed in Boswell's ground-breaking biography of Johnson. Scotland, like that young man, was being offered an opportunity that would help the nation see its potential.

The national circumstances in the decades following the Act of Union were transformative for the people of Scotland. They were the junior partner in the relationship, but this position afforded them much personal freedom. Aside from subduing the diminishing threat of Jacobinism, England left Scotland largely to her own devices. The Scots enjoyed a strong government that didn't bother to interfere as long as order remained.

The short-term trade-offs of the union turned into long-term benefits. In the 1720s, grain exports doubled. The greatest problem of Lowland farmers was not famine but surplus. Glasgow merchants began trading with the American colonies and were running the lucrative tobacco trade by the mid-1700s. William Mackintosh of Borlum, the Jacobite leader imprisoned in Edinburgh Castle, observed in 1729 that the middle class was better dressed, furnished, and housed than they'd ever been. It was this, perhaps more than anything else, that doomed the risings of 1715 and 1745. Middle-class Scotland had no good reason to overthrow the English yoke. They were too busy gaining wealth and increasing their standard of living.

It was in this changing world that several important thinkers emerged. One was Francis Hutcheson, a soft-spoken clergyman and teacher. Another was Henry Home, Lord Kames, a rough-and-tumble lawyer and judge. Separately, they would spawn the Scottish Enlightenment and inspire a generation to a new understanding of humanity. The great books of Scotland and the Enlightenment in general include Hutcheson's *System of Moral Philosophy* and Kames' *Sketches of the History of Man*. From these works came the works of David Hume, Adam Smith, William Robertson, Adam Ferguson, and Thomas Reid— what we today call the social sciences. Among so many things, the Scottish Enlightenment produced the *Encyclopedia Britannica*, which was first published in Edinburgh in 1768. And, from the name of that encyclopedia, we can see the mindset of this new generation: they were British above all else.

Francis Hutcheson

Francis Hutcheson was born in Northern Ireland, an Ulster Scot or what we today would call Scots-Irish, but he was thoroughly Scottish in upbringing, religion, and outlook. After attending the University of Glasgow, he went to Dublin in 1718 and there joined a circle of intellects surrounding Robert (Viscount) Molesworth. From them, he absorbed the works of English luminaries John Locke, Isaac Newton, Samuel Clarke, Jonathan Swift, and Anthony Ashley Cooper, 3rd Earl of Shaftesbury.

Hutcheson developed a concept of humanity far removed from the fire and brimstone of John Knox and the Kirk, though still rooted in Christianity. He believed that everyone is born with a sense of right and wrong. Moral reasoning is expressed through our emotions, and the most important of these is love, particularly love for others. Everyone's goal is happiness, which is obtained by making others happy. In 1725, Hutcheson published his first book, *An Inquiry into the Original of Our Ideas of Beauty and Virtue*. It was an instant success.

Hutcheson found a patron in Archibald Campbell (Lord Ilay), whose father had beaten the Earl of Mar at Sheriffmuir and was a staunch Whig. With Ilay's help, Hutcheson was placed at the University of Glasgow in the Chair of Moral Philosophy. There, Hutcheson influenced a generation of thinkers, including a young student named Adam Smith, who came to Glasgow in 1737.

Hutcheson explained that the crucial element to allowing the good nature of humanity to spread was liberty. Human beings, he explained, are born free and equal. These are "right" and universal, meaning they should be enjoyed by everyone regardless of social position or even gender. The worst crime against these rights was slavery, which Hutcheson greatly opposed. He died in 1746 as Bonnie Prince Charlie was fleeing to the continent.

Henry Home, Lord Kames

Henry Home was the son of a gentleman from Kames, in Berwickshire. He was raised Episcopalian and became an advocate (lawyer) and a member of the Scottish Bar in 1723. In 1737, Lord Kames found a position as curator of the Advocates Library and turned the institution into a repository for books on many subjects that helped spawn the Enlightenment in Edinburgh. When he became a judge in 1752, he chose the title Lord Kames, derived from the name of his family home.

Lord Kames surrounded himself with bright young academics, including John Miller, Adam Smith, James Boswell, and David Hume. Hume was particularly close to Lord Kames, who was like a father figure to the young philosopher. Yet, like father and son, they often quarreled, especially concerning faith.

Lord Kames' contribution to Enlightenment thinking was mainly in the realm of history. He was also a founding member of the Philosophical Society of Edinburgh. Kames, being a judge, was particularly interested in the reason for laws and government. He proposed that human communities progressed through four distinct stages based largely on the way they obtained and kept their property. First came hunting and fishing, then herding (which led to animal domestication), and then agriculture, which occasioned the creation of laws to protect that individual property. Lastly came commercial society, where men bought and sold goods. This required even more complicated systems of laws concerning contracts and loans. Commerce, like Hutcheson's liberty, led to more human interactions. These interactions refined and polished the manners of humanity, leading to a more sophisticated "gentleman" who would be likely to express the selflessness within his heart. Commercial society was also known as *capitalism*, and this was the only stage at which Kames thought Hutcheson's natural altruism could thrive.

Kames' four-stage theory of societies was at once liberating and oppressive. It caused the modern mind to see change not as something terrifying but as something beneficial to the natural progress of society. However, his theory also helped feed racial stereotypes about the "savage" and "uncivilized" societies that were not commercial, according to this Scottish model. Kame continued to write and work as a judge for the rest of his life. He died naturally at the age of eighty-seven.

James Boswell

Boswell grew up in Edinburgh, the son of the judge Lord Auchinleck. He was mentored by Lord Kames, who encouraged his intellectual and literary interests. He left his home city and arrived in London in 1760 at age twenty. There he found that his greatest hindrance to success was his native land. The new King George III had selected a Scotsman, Lord Bute, as prime minister, and Bute turned out to be very unpopular. It was not a good time to be a Scot or to speak not only with an accent but in a very different form of Anglo-Saxon English (then called Scots). Self-conscious Scottish noblemen and ladies attended lectures and took classes to speak more like the English.

However, Boswell's first trip to London was an escape from the University of Glasgow, where he was attending lectures by Adam Smith. Boswell's father brought him back to school, and after passing his law exam, he returned to London with his father's permission.

In 1763, Boswell met Samuel Johnson, one of the greatest writers of the English language. The two became friends, though Boswell saw Johnson as something of a father figure. In 1764, Boswell began his Grand Tour of Europe, staying a year in Germany and then traveling to Switzerland, Italy, Corsica, and France. On this trip, he met other giants of the Enlightenment, including Jean-Jacques Rousseau and Voltaire. In 1766, he returned home and completed his study in law at the University of Edinburgh, becoming an advocate.

Boswell's contributions to the Enlightenment and Western civilization were not completely apparent while he was alive, but in his last years, he completed his masterwork, *Life of Samuel Johnson*, a biography of his friend. Many consider it to be the greatest biography in the English language. The book was published in 1791 and became an instant critical and commercial success. (Johnson had died in 1784.) The book was unlike any biography before it. Boswell used quotations that he had written down directly from Johnson. Instead of providing a simple fact-based summary of Johnson's life, he provided an intimate portrayal of the writer. Boswell also kept extensive journals throughout his life, and these detailed accounts of his life, thoughts, travels, and interactions with some of the most important people of his time have been a wealth of information for later historians.

Adam Smith

Born in 1723, the son of an advocate, Adam Smith entered the University of Glasgow when he was fourteen. There, Smith came under the spell of Francis Hutcheson and developed his interest in reason, liberties, and the rights of man, with a particular interest in economics. He would, like many of his fellow students, refer to their mentor as "the never to be forgotten Hutcheson."

Smith went on to study at Oxford but found the university stifling. The greatest benefit of his studies there was the use of the extensive Bodleian Library. Under the patronage of Lord Kames, he began delivering lectures at the University of Edinburgh after graduating.

In 1751, Smith took a position teaching logic at Glasgow University. The next year, he was made a member of the Philosophical Society of Edinburgh. In 1759, he published *The Theory of Moral Sentiments*, which provided many of the philosophical foundations of his later works. This book garnered Smith a lot of attention, and he became a favorite teacher in Glasgow.

In 1762, he was offered the job of tutoring Henry Scott, the young Duke of Buccleuch. This allowed him to travel throughout Europe. In Paris, he met the diplomat Benjamin Franklin. After four years, Smith's tutoring assignment ended, and he returned to Scotland to work on his greatest work, *An Inquiry into the Nature and Causes of the Wealth of Nations,* published in 1776.

This book, often shortened to *The Wealth of Nations*, would prove exceptionally influential, especially in the world of economics. It was a paradigm shift, moving away from the *mercantilism* of the past and focusing on a new system to understand the growing commercial societies that Kame had identified as the last stage of civilization.

Smith noted, among many things, the importance of the division of labor to increase production. He explained that the wages for labor depend upon competition among laborers and masters. He explained how workers could combine and no longer compete and that this would drive wages up. When masters combined (which he explained happened much more than people believed), wages decreased. He warned against the influence of special interest groups to stifle a nation's economy. His work, though laborious on occasion, became the gold standard of classic economics and took its place among books that can safely be said to have changed the world.

The book was a commercial success, which surprised many in Smith's circles. Hume declared it was excellent but too hard for the common reader. Edward Gibbon wrote to Adam Ferguson to exclaim about Smith's work. On the other hand, the *Annual Register* gave Smith's book a negative review. In 1791, the radical Thomas Paine wrote in the *Rights of Man* that the reviewer, believed to be the Whig Edmund Burke, simply lacked the talent to understand the book.

In the years after the publication, Smith was consulted by the British Parliament on economic matters, such as the implementation of new taxes. Smith was praised by Prime Minister William Pitt in 1792, though by then Smith had been dead for two years. The *mercantilism* of the past had given way to the free market vision of Smith and other economists. This attitude was adopted by the British government and helped fuel the expansion of the country's economy during the Industrial Revolution. Smith's common-sense approach to economics is said to have been the reason for his great success but also limited his theories. While Smith was among the first economists, many in economics today believe his ideas are outdated.

David Hume

David Hume was born in 1711 in Edinburgh, spending much of his time at Ninewells, his family's small estate in the borderlands. His father died when he was only two, and his mother became entirely focused on rearing her three children. Seeing promise in her youngest son, Katherine Hume sent not just her older son but young David to the University of Edinburgh when he was only ten.

While his family thought he should go into law, Hume decided instead to be a scholar and philosopher. After a rigorous self-imposed routine of reading and reflection for three years, Hume had a breakthrough that first alarmed him and then set him on his course. He moved to France, where he could live cheaply. He settled in a small village in Anjou, which housed a Jesuit school. Having abandoned the religious teachings of his family and the Kirk, he baited the Jesuits with arguments against their faith.

In his twenty-third year, Hume began writing *A Treatise of Human Nature*. He returned to England in 1737 with his manuscript complete and ready for print. To get it printed, he removed some of the more controversial sections that criticized Christianity. The book was not a great success, and Hume felt like he had failed. He applied for the Chair of Ethics and Pneumatic (Mental) Philosophy at Edinburgh in 1745 but was rejected. Six years later, he was rejected for the Chair of Logic in Glasgow. He would never hold an academic post. The next year, Hume became secretary to his cousin, Lt. General James St. Clair, a role that took him to Austria and Italy.

Humes had more success with later publications, including *An Enquiry Concerning Human Understanding*, *An Enquiry Concerning the Principles of Morals*, and a collection of essays titled *Political Discourses*. Many of these were reworkings of parts he'd taken out of *Treatise*.

He then became the Librarian to the Edinburgh Faculty of Advocates, like Lord Kame before him. Using the library's resources he compiled a book in six volumes. *The History of England* appeared in installments from 1754 to 1762. This became a bestseller and gave him financial independence. Still, he was a known atheist and skeptic and faced charges of excommunication from the Kirk and dismissal from his position.

In 1763, Hume accepted a job as the secretary to the ambassador to France. He became a hit in Parisian salons for his wit, love of good food, and delight in the affections of women. He returned to Scotland and moved into a comfortable house in New Town in Edinburgh. He spent his remaining years editing his works and enjoying the company of friends and acquaintances. In 1775, he was diagnosed with intestinal cancer and arranged for the posthumous publication of a controversial work called *Dialogues Concerning Natural Religion*.

Hume's influence in the realm of philosophy can hardly be understated. Many regard him as one of the greatest philosophers in the English language and one of the most influential in Europe. Many approaches and ideas in philosophy carry the title "Humean," as being influenced or directly pulled from Hume's works. Humes' thoughts on religion and use of rationalism influenced German theology during the German Enlightenment. Hume's *Treatise* has been called the founding document on cognitive science. Immanuel Kant credited Hume with awakening him from his "dogmatic slumber," and Albert Einstein credited Hume's works in helping him create his theory of special relativity. However, Hume's writings on race led to the David Hume Tower of Edinburgh University being renamed by a student-led campaign. Hume was a great philosopher and writer, but like so many historical figures, his views in certain areas failed to age gracefully.

Chapter 9: The Industrial Revolution and Its Impact on Scottish Society

When America won its independence from Britain, the former colony took control of its tobacco trade. Thus, Scotland's near monopoly disappeared overnight. In its place, Scottish merchants focused on the cotton industry. Raw cotton was purchased from the American South and processed in Scotland.

One of the earliest forms of industrialization was the power loom, an automated loom invented by Englishman Edmund Cartwright, which could weave cotton into textiles at an astonishing rate. This allowed the Scottish merchants to sell huge quantities of cotton in a short amount of time.

Cartwright's first mill was built in 1788 and was run by steam power. This revolutionary invention was perfected by James Watt, born in Greenock, Scotland, in 1736. The steam water pump had been invented in the seventeenth century, and the first successful engine was developed by Thomas Newcomen in 1712, but Watt's invention greatly improved the engine to allow it to be utilized in a myriad of different ways. His work on the steam engine turned it from a small novelty to the force behind the industrial revolution.

The Boulton-Watt engine, named after Watt and Matthew Boulton, who supported the inventor's years of trial and error, was first used as a pump for mines in 1776. Watt improved his invention again, and in 1782, a Boulton-Watt engine was used at a sawmill, where it replaced twelve horses. Watt also created the concept of "horsepower," meaning the sawmill engine had twelve horsepower. By 1800, eight-four British cotton mills used Boulton-Watt engines. Soon, steam engines based on Watt's design were used to turn paddles, creating steamboats. Then steam engines were used to produce locomotives and begin the railroad industry.

James Watt, Scottish inventor.
https://commons.wikimedia.org/wiki/File:James_Watt_by_Henry_Howard.jpg

Watt was an undeniable genius. While still quite young, he attracted the attention of Glasgow professors Joseph Black, the famed chemist, and the equally well-known Adam Smith, who both became Watt's friends and supporters. Watt also invented the pounds per square inch (psi), which is still used today to measure pressure. The "watt," a unit of power, is named after the inventor. He was one of the first people to create and use bleach to whiten textiles. Watt was a member of the Lunar Society of Birmingham, which was a dinner club of industrialists and other important figures at the beginning of the Industrial Revolution. He retired in 1800, a relatively wealthy man.

The cotton industry in Scotland would eventually be eclipsed by iron, steel, coal, engineering, and shipbuilding. The area along the River Clyde soon became a world leader in shipbuilding. Bridges and canals were built to ease the movement of goods and people.

While Scotland became more industrialized, Scottish farmers also looked to new methods for raising crops and livestock. In the Highlands, the previous attempts to undermine the clan system had been largely successful. Clan chiefs turned into landlords who found the best use of their land was keeping herds of sheep. They evicted many of their residents. Whole villages were depopulated, and the ousted Highlanders had little choice but to immigrate to America or join the growing populations of Scottish cities. Within the cities, numbers were drastically rising. Glasgow, home to only 12,000 people in 1707, had a population of 77,000 by 1810 and 300,000 by 1830. In 1760, Edinburgh had a population of 50,000. Forty years later, that number had doubled.

It was not just Highlanders flocking to cities but also Irish immigrants looking for more opportunities and later fleeing the potato famine of the 1840s. These industrialized urban centers became overcrowded and led to appalling living conditions that directly affected the health of the population. Disease ran rampant. Mortality rates soared. The influx of laborers, as Adam Smith would have predicted, caused a drop in wages.

By the end of the eighteenth century, driven by the threat of power looms and steam engines that put them out of their jobs, Scottish cotton weavers formed one of the first trade unions. However, it wasn't until later in the nineteenth century that the trade union movement really took off. The Scottish Miners' Federation was founded in 1886. Around the same time, the Scottish Labor Party was formed, with one of its stated aims being home rule for Scotland. It did not last long and was absorbed into the larger British Labor Party.

The ideals of the Enlightenment were not abandoned during the Industrial Revolution. One of the greatest proponents of Francis Hutcheson and Adam Smith in the early nineteenth century was the University of Edinburgh Professor Dugald Stewart. Stewart was a popular and influential teacher, but he is perhaps best known for who he taught. Some of his pupils were Francis Horner, Francis Jeffery, Henry Thomas Cockburn, Henry Brougham, and the Englishman Sydney Smith. Several of these individuals would have stunning political careers as prime ministers and lord chancellors. In fact, for part of the nineteenth century, the British Parliament was dominated by Scotsmen.

Yet, what this group did before embarking on their political careers is what they might be best known for: the creation of the *Edinburgh Review*, or more accurately, the third version of the *Edinburgh Review*. This magazine, which ran from 1802 to 1929, was a great promoter of Whig or liberal politics and Romanticism. It could be highly critical, especially to the Lake Poets, including William Wordsworth. The *Review* was an instant success and helped launch the careers of many great writers, including William Makepeace Thackeray, William Hazlitt, John Stuart Mill, and the greatest writer of the age (and a former student of Dugald Stewart), Sir Walter Scott.

Born in 1771 in Edinburgh's Old Town, Walter Scott was the ninth son of an advocate. He contracted polio when he was young, which gave him a life-long limp. Shortly thereafter, he was sent to live with his grandparents thirty miles outside of Edinburgh. There, he regained his health and became enamored with reading and hearing Scottish legends from his aunt Jenny and grandmother Barbara. He began writing poetry.

Scott returned to Edinburgh in 1778, where his family was now living in a larger house in New Town. He attended the high school and received tutoring in writing and arithmetic. He went to live with his Aunt Jenny again for a few months in Kelso and there met a good friend and future business partner, James Ballantyne. He attended the University of Edinburgh and eventually decided to study law. He then met the great Scottish poet, Robert Burns.

Scott completed his studies in 1792 and began working as a lawyer while translating German poems into English in his spare time. In 1809, he joined Ballantyne as a silent partner in a publishing house, John Ballantyne & Co. Through this publishing house, Scott began to publish poems, notably *Lady of the Lake*. In 1808, he published *Marmion* about the battle between the English and Scots at Flodden Field in 1513. This contained one of his most often quoted phrases, "Oh! What a tangled web we weave/ when first we practice to deceive!"

In 1814, his first novel, *Waverley*, was published anonymously. The book was a great success, and he followed it up with more in the series, though each was published under a pseudonym. Most people began to suspect that Scott was the author, but he did not publicly acknowledge the fact until 1827.

In 1818, the prince regent (later George IV) was so impressed with Scott's talents that he allowed the writer to search Edinburgh Castle for the lost royal Scottish regalia, last seen after the passing of the Act of Union of 1707. Scott eventually found the regalia in an oak chest, wrapped in linen just as they had been over a hundred years before. Scott was awarded a baronet and was heavily involved in planning George IV's visit to Scotland in 1820, the first visit from a Hanoverian monarch.

Scott continued writing, producing international bestsellers like *Ivanhoe*, *Rob Roy*, and *The Heart of Midlothian*. He became one of the most popular writers of his time and is often credited with inventing historical fiction. He became an exemplar of European Romanticism and became a force for preserving a mythical version of Scottish history that seemed to criticize the industrialization and urbanization of the country during the nineteenth century. At the very least, Scott offered his readers a romantic version of Scottish history.

It was during the period just before and after Scott's works that the "Clearances" of the Highlands took place. As previously mentioned, clan chieftains took on the role of landlords and found it was more lucrative to keep sheep than people, evicting large numbers of people from their ancestral lands. They were sent to coastal villages, where they were expected to fish, gather kelp to sell, or farm much smaller plots of land called crofts. It soon became apparent that there was not enough work in these crofting villages, and many people had no choice but to emigrate either to Scottish cities or, more often, North America—especially Nova Scotia. The Highland society that Scott had popularized in his works was quickly disappearing, if it had even really existed at all. Later, the Highland Potato Famine finalized the Clearances.

Still, the country, especially the Lowlands, provided fertile ground for the Industrial Revolution. There was abundant and cheap labor available. Scottish banks were more lightly regulated than their English counterparts, and this allowed for tremendous financial growth.

Scotland enjoyed a large coastline, and almost every area of the country was easily reachable via ships, canals, roads, and eventually railroads. Scotland employed the use of turnpikes, where private companies could build roads and charge reasonable tolls for their use. This resulted in a wide network of maintained roads that could be used for transport.

Scottish merchants traded in a wide variety of commodities, including leather, sugar, rope, and linen goods. They bought sugar from plantations in the West Indies and sold it to dealers in Britain for high prices thanks to the skyrocketing demand. Factories in Scotland included glassworks, iron foundries, and sailmakers. There were breweries, whisky distilleries, and soap makers as well.

Coal mining became a major industry. Scotland went from producing one million tons of coal out of five different coal fields in 1775 to over three million in 1830. Production would peak at 142 million tons per year in the twentieth century. By 1860, Scotland contained 171 iron furnaces and produced over a million tons of pig iron a year.

The first railroad in Scotland was between Monkland and Kirkintilloch, built in 1826. In the 1840s, railway building increased dramatically, putting Scotland in competition with its southern neighbor for the number of lines and services. The North British Railway connected eastern Scotland with Newcastle, and the Caledonian Railway connected Glasgow and Carlisle. By the 1860s, a series of mergers meant that five companies owned 98 percent of the rail lines in Scotland.

In 1850, 32 percent of Scotland's population lived in a city. By 1900, 50 percent of the population was urban. Glasgow had become the largest city with a population approaching one million by 1900. It was one of the largest cities in the world and was considered the "Second City of the Empire" after London. Dundee, on the east coast of Scotland, emerged as an urban center thanks to an expanded harbor and the growth of the three main industries of the city: jute, jam, and journalism. The jam specifically refers to marmalade, which was first commercially made in Dundee in the eighteenth century.

Yet, in Dundee, Glasgow, Aberdeen, and other growing cities, living conditions continued to decline. Infant mortality was much higher in Scottish cities during the Industrial Revolution than in English or other European cities. Overall mortality was also exceptionally high. The death rate was at its highest in the 1840s due to an influx of Irish immigrants and Highlanders escaping the potato famines. This was finally curbed thanks to advancements in medicine.

In fact, Scotland had a long history of medical developments, beginning with John and William Hunter, brothers from Calderwood in East Kilbride. Surgeons, physicians, and anatomists, the brothers helped advance medicine in Britain—largely due to the availability of human cadavers for dissection. The use of cadavers was not frowned upon in Scotland as it was in England. This eventually led to great discoveries but also the infamous case of Burke and Hare, who murdered victims to provide bodies to Dr. Knox in Edinburgh in the 1820s.

One of the more famous Scottish physicians of the nineteenth century was Sir Charles Bell. Born in Edinburgh in 1774, Charles came from a distinguished family of surgeons and lawyers. He was also another student of Dugald Stewart. Charles was forced to leave Edinburgh and go to London due to a feud one of his older brothers had with faculty members of the University of Edinburgh. Bell joined the Hunterian School of Medicine founded by William Hunter. He was present at the Battle of Waterloo, where he acted as a battlefield surgeon. He used his artistic abilities to give new insight into the inner workings of the body as well as many illnesses and how they affected his patients.

Charles Bell is not to be confused with Benjamin Bell, an associate of John Hunter and Scottish physician William Cullen. Benjamin, born in Dumfries in 1749, was the first scientific Scottish surgeon and founded a dynasty of doctors, including his great-grandson, Joseph Bell. Joseph was renowned for his diagnostic abilities and regularly astonished his pupils, including a young Arthur Conan Doyle, who used Dr. Bell as the basis for the character of Sherlock Holmes.

Perhaps one of the most interesting narratives of Scotland in the Industrial Revolution began with a man named George Lauder, who was born in Dunfermline in 1815. George's father owned a snuff mill, and when George became an adult, he started a general store on High Street in his hometown. George was a Chartist, which meant he believed in universal suffrage for all male citizens of the United Kingdom. This was a working-class movement named after the People's Charter of 1838. At the time, only landowners could vote. This excluded a huge swath of the population, especially disenfranchised urban voters.

George was also a champion of education rights for all Scots and was closely aligned with radical liberals like his father-in-law, the firebrand Thomas Morrison. He was also a Scottish nationalist. George had only one child, a son named George Lauder Jr. He also helped to support and educate his two nephews, Andrew and Thomas. His son was very close to his cousin Andrew, and the two grew like brothers. However, when Andrew was twelve, his family had to borrow money from George Lauder Sr. and immigrate to Allegheny, Pennsylvania.

In America, Andrew began to work to help support his family, first at a Scottish-owned cotton mill and then as a messenger boy in a telegraph office. This young Scottish-born boy, whose full name was Andrew Carnegie, was beginning a journey that would lead him to become one of the world's wealthiest men. He would later make his cousin, George Lauder Jr., a partner in his businesses.

However, Carnegie did not forget the lessons learned in his uncle's general store. Knowing the difference that a helping hand could make, he spent much of his fortune on philanthropic works. He drew inspiration from the tales of William Wallace, Robert Bruce, and Rob Roy. He understood the importance of education and built libraries in countless towns across America. However, what his uncle might have thought of his exploitation of workers is unknown.

Chapter 10: Modern Scotland— Devolution, National Identity, and the Quest for Independence

Since the Act of Union in 1707, many Scots have dreamed of an independent Scotland.

The urbanization, growth, and industrialization of Scotland led to a government crisis in the management of Scottish affairs by the authorities of Great Britain. Certain agencies were created to deal with the pressing needs of the Scottish population, including the Board of Supervision for Poor Relief (created in 1845), the General Board of Commissioners in Lunacy (1857), and the Scottish Education Department as part of the Privy Council (1872).

However, these agencies had little oversight and accountability. Scottish MPs requested that the British government create a Secretary of Scotland, which was finally created in 1885 as the Scottish Office, run by the Secretary of State of Scotland. Under this new office, various government bodies were consolidated and reformed to better serve the Scottish population, which continued to increase. (The year 1901 brought the highest increase of 10 percent.) By the early twentieth century, boards of health, agriculture, and prisons were created by the Reorganization of Offices Act of 1928.

Still, the advocates of home rule were not satisfied. In 1907, another small step was taken in the creation of the Scottish Committee in the

House of Commons. Scottish members could deal with Scottish bills that might be presented to the whole legislative body.

With the outbreak of war in 1914, Scotland's problems seemed less pressing, and Scots answered the call to support the United Kingdom on every front of the war effort. There were thirty-five Scottish battalions in World War I. They served on the Western Front, in Egypt, in Palestine, and in defending Britain. There were the Highlanders and The Royal Scots, among others.

The toll that the war took on the Scottish people was severe. In some cases, all the male members of a single family were wiped out throughout the war. The exact number of Scots who died in World War I is not yet known, but it is believed to be over one hundred thousand. It was not just the war that claimed Scots but the outbreak of an influenza pandemic misleadingly called the "Spanish flu." Scotland had a period of high death rates and decreased birth and marriage rates as a result. Still, Scotland's population reached a record of 4.8 million in 1919. At the same time, the end of the war led to a "baby boom," and 1920 holds the record for the most births in a single year at 137,000.

The interwar period for Scotland did not bring the boom and bust of the United States or Germany but the perhaps more tragic dismantling of the economy. Generally, economic growth was slow in the United Kingdom after the First World War, but it was especially sluggish in Scotland. Wages and salaries barely increased in the 1920s. After the onset of the global Great Depression in 1929, Scottish incomes fell drastically. Unemployment skyrocketed in Scotland and quickly outpaced the rest of the United Kingdom. Scotland was also slower to recover. In 1934, for instance, Great Britain had an estimated unemployment rate of 16.6 percent, which is certainly high. In the same year, Scotland had an unemployment rate of 23.2 percent, and its rate did not return to the 1929 figures until 1936, four years after the rest of the country.

It has been speculated that the reason for this downturn was Scotland's reliance on heavy industry and a lack of diversification among its industries. However, research has shown that Scotland's industries were just as diversified as England's, the main difference being Scotland's much slower growth. The reality was more complicated. Scotland had a large number of jobs in declining or depressed industries that were particularly susceptible to economic distress. One example is shipbuilding, which was much more important in Scotland than in England or Wales. When the demand for ships rapidly decreased after World War I, Scotland was hit especially hard. Since many other industries in Scotland also relied on business from shipbuilders and their employees, they suffered as well.

Scotland's population growth also suffered at this time. In fact, from 1921 to 1931, the population decreased by 0.9 percent. This was the first recorded drop in the country's population since the first census records of the early nineteenth century.

Many Scots blamed London for their woes, and the idea of home rule was revived. London responded with another small step by making the Scottish Secretary a Cabinet rank with wider powers. Scotland thus gained more administrative independence, but the new Nationalists wanted nothing less than complete political independence.

In 1934, the Scottish National Party was formed from the merger of two nationalist groups. The party had been conceived by John MacCormick, a lawyer from the University of Glasgow who wanted to raise the question of home rule above party loyalties in Scotland. The movement had strong support and strong leadership. The first presidents of the party were James Graham, 6th Duke of Montrose, and Robert Cunninghame Graham. Montrose was a naval officer and politician who was the first to take a photo of a solar eclipse and is credited with the invention of the aircraft carrier. Graham, who was not related to the duke, was an adventurer and socialist politician. Both men were keenly devoted to Scottish home rule. However, events on the continent in 1939 would once again undermine the home rule cause.

The Nationalists did not want Scotland to be a completely independent state. "Home rule" was a phrase used to indicate a political situation in which Scotland would have autonomy to govern itself while remaining part of the United Kingdom and receiving the protections the UK offered. This meant that when World War II broke out in 1939, most Scottish men expected to fight for Great Britain against her enemies. One of the Scottish National Party leaders, Douglas Young, argued that Scottish people should refuse conscription into the armed forces. But he was vilified for undermining the war effort and thus helping the Axis powers. Young was imprisoned for his beliefs.

John MacCormick left the party in 1942 because he could not steer the SNP to home rule, which was believed to be supported by most

Scottish people. The SNP instead adopted the more radical position of complete independence from the UK. MacCormick argued for a "devolved" Scottish Assembly and formed the Scottish Covenant Association. (Devolution is the statutory delegation of powers from a central government to a more local level. It is often compared to the concept of home rule in Scotland.)The name of the Scottish Covenant Association was chosen to directly reference the Covenanters of the sixteenth and seventeenth centuries.

Like their forefathers, the association created a new Scottish Covenant to be signed by the public, this time in support of devolution. Written in 1949 at the Church of Scotland Assembly Halls in Edinburgh, the document was eventually signed by over two million people—a little less than half the population of Scotland. However, the petition had little political impact.

In the 1960s, support for Home Rule gained support in political circles. Finally, in 1978, the Scotland Act was passed, which would establish a devolved legislative body in Scotland as long as it was approved by 40 percent of the Scottish electorate. A consequent referendum, however, failed to produce the needed votes. The proposed Scottish Assembly was not created, and the act was repealed.

This might have been the end of the idea of home rule, but there was still a strong current within Scottish society that longed for the authority to at least partially govern themselves. This finally came with the Scotland Act of 1998, which was supported by a referendum held in 1997 showing that most Scots were in favor of home rule. This act created a new Scottish Parliament within Scotland with legislative and taxing powers. It was the most significant piece of legislation for Scotland since the Act of Union in 1707.

The Scottish Parliament meets in the Holyrood area of Edinburgh and is often called "Holyrood" for that reason. There are 129 democratically elected members of the parliament. The Scottish National Party, as of 2021, holds the plurality of seats.

In line with this new independence, the Stone of Scone was finally returned to Scotland in 1996 in acknowledgment of Scottish heritage and the cultural significance of the object. Interestingly, the stone had been stolen from England by Scottish Nationalists in 1950 but returned four months later—though some suggest the stone returned was not the original stone. The stone was brought out in 2023 for the crowning of

King Charles III.

Another possible reason for the change of public opinion on home rule from the early 1970s to the 1990s was the discovery of oil in the North Sea off the coast of Scotland in the mid-1970s. The Scottish National Party pushed hard with the slogan "It's Scotland's oil," attempting to convince the public that the Scottish people would not enjoy the benefits of the oil without a devolved legislative body. It is also worth noting that, over time, the SNP stepped back from its position on complete independence. This also helped lead to the creation of the Scottish Parliament.

While Scottish population growth has not boomed in the twenty-first century, the population enjoys a steady growth rate. The heavy industries of the Industrial Revolution have not made a comeback in the country, but new industries have begun. Silicon Glen is a high-tech sector of businesses from Dundee to Edinburgh and Inverclyde, including Stirling, Glasgow, and Fife.

The development of Silicon Glen hails back to post-World War II when Ferranti moved an electronic plant to Edinburgh. Silicon Glen produced semiconductors, largely in Glenrothes. The sector was hit hard by the technology collapse of 2000, but Scotland had learned from previous eras. Thanks to the diversification of industries, the country was not largely affected. Since then, Silicon Glen has bounced back, with plants being built by foreign companies like Amazon and the development of local businesses.

While Scotland's future is unknown, there remains reason to be hopeful.

Conclusion

While it is a small nation, roughly equivalent in size to the US state of South Carolina, Scotland has had a great impact on Europe and the rest of the world. Over the years, many Scots have emigrated to places like the United States, Canada, Australia, and New Zealand. There are many more people of Scottish descent living abroad than the five million that call Scotland home.

In the same way, Scotland's ideas and inventions have spread around the world. The Church of Scotland is in every Presbyterian church. The principles of liberty and self-governance that Scottish thinkers first expressed have become the cornerstones of other nations' constitutions. Scots have contributed the pedal bicycle and the pneumatic tire, the condensing steam engine of James Watt, the first iron-hulled ship, wire rope, the telephone (Alexander Graham Bell was born in Scotland), the BBC, radar, postcards, modern economics, modern geology, the hypodermic syringe, and fried chicken. In the world of domestic appliances, the Scots seemed particularly adept at inventing not just the refrigerator but also the flush toilet, the lawnmower, and the television.

While Scotland struggled after 1707 to regain its independence from England, one could easily argue that in the intervening years, Scottish politicians, businessmen, and writers slowly conquered their southern neighbor without the need for an army.

There is reason to believe, with the current state of affairs, that the Scottish people will be content with their situation. However, a study of Scottish history tells any student who is paying attention that the Scots are never idle for long. They will, one way or another, make themselves known. Scots tend to come onto the scene, whether through art or science, industry or politics, and solve a problem that has been troubling people for generations or, perhaps, introduce a problem that no one was even aware of. This is one of the lasting benefits of Scotland and the Scottish people. Their rich heritage and their desire for liberty—however they might define it—drives them to prove themselves repeatedly, and the world is often, but not always, the better for it.

While it is easy to get lost in the triumphs of Scotland, like the fight for independence from England, or its romantic failures, like the tale of Bonnie Prince Charlie, we must not forget that Scotland carries the stains of the era of colonization. Scottish merchants traded in human beings, and many Scottish immigrants to British colonies waged merciless war on indigenous people. However, Scotland shows every indication of carrying this shame honorably. In keeping with the strange nature of the country, Scots can also empathize with those they helped to conquer because they themselves were conquered many times. Scotland's history is that of a country oppressed but regularly breaking through that oppression by force, will, or wit alone.

Think of the Highlanders—not the Hollywood version, but the real thing. They lived a mean existence, but they could trace their line back to noble blood. It is hard not to like a group of self-reliant people who spend their time fighting each other over every slight but, when an outside force threatens their homes, come together to send the invaders running. Even in defeat, they can fade into the mountains and glens, only to regroup and continue the fight.

The Lowlander, not often celebrated in verse or on the big screen, is just as appealing. Often, they were hard workers with an appreciation for equal education, through which the lowest laborer could often quote Latin or at least read and write. From their numbers came some of the greatest thinkers of the Enlightenment who truly reshaped the world with words and ideas. Poets, novelists, dukes, tinkerers, and merchants who could buy and sell them all, all called Scotland home.

From the clear waters of mountain rivers to the dirty streets of Victorian Edinburgh, Scotland has managed to enchant many people the world over. Her history tells a story of struggle, failure, and triumph that resonates with any breathing person. This book is just a small portion of the great history of the country. We hope it encourages you to investigate the history of Scotland even further.

If you enjoyed this book, a review on Amazon would be greatly appreciated because it would mean a lot to hear from you.

To leave a review:

1. Open your camera app.
2. Point your mobile device at the QR code.
3. The review page will appear in your web browser.

Thanks for your support!

Here's another book by Enthralling History that you might like

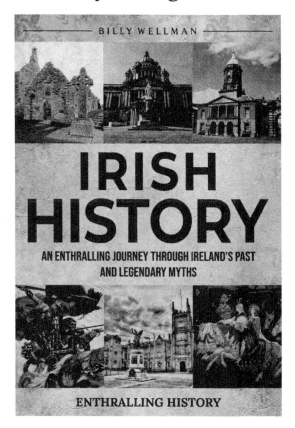

Free limited time bonus

We forget 90% of everything that we've read in 7 days...

Get the free printable pdf summary of the book you've read AND much, much more... shhhh...

Enter Your Most Frequently Used Email to Get Started

DOWNLOAD FREE PDF SUMMARY

© Enthralling History

Stop for a moment. We have a free bonus set up for you. The problem is this: we forget 90% of everything that we read after 7 days. Crazy fact, right? Here's the solution: we've created a printable, 1-page pdf summary for this book that you're reading now. All you have to do to get your free pdf summary is to go to the following website: https://livetolearn.lpages.co/enthrallinghistory/

Or, Scan the QR code!

Once you do, it will be intuitive. Enjoy, and thank you!

Bibliography

"The Battle of Stirling Bridge." *National Wallace Monument*, https://www.nationalwallacemonument.com/the-battle-of-stirling-bridge/. Accessed 8 November 2023.

Buxton, Neil. "Economic Growth in Scotland between the wars." *The Economic History Review*, vol. 33, no. 4, 1980, pp. 538-55. *JSTOR*.

Clarkson, Tim. *The Picts: A History*. Birlinn, Limited, 2016.

"Edmund Cartwright | Lemelson." *Lemelson-MIT*, https://lemelson.mit.edu/resources/edmund-cartwright. Accessed 4 December 2023.

Herman, Arthur. *How the Scots Invented the Modern World: The True Story of How Western Europe's Poorest Nation Created Our World & Everything In It*. MJF Books, 2001.

Lira, Carl. "Watt Biography." *MSU College of Engineering*, https://www.egr.msu.edu/~lira/supp/steam/wattbio.html. Accessed 4 December 2023.

Maclean, Fitzroy, and Magnus Linklater. *Scotland: a concise history*. Thames & Hudson, 2000.

Morris, William Edward, and Charlotte R. Brown. "David Hume (Stanford Encyclopedia of Philosophy)." *Stanford Encyclopedia of Philosophy*, 26 February 2001, https://plato.stanford.edu/entries/hume/#LifeWork. Accessed 26 November 2023.

"North Berwick harbour severely damaged by huge waves." *BBC*, 30 October 2023, https://www.bbc.com/news/uk-scotland-edinburgh-east-fife-67259624. Accessed 30 October 2023.

"Scotland's People and the First World War." *National Records of Scotland,* https://www.nrscotland.gov.uk/research/learning/first-world-war/scotlands-people-and-the-first-world-war. Accessed 12 December 2023.

"Scots abroad: medical influences in the 18th century." *Royal College of Physicians of Edinburgh,* https://www.rcpe.ac.uk/heritage/scots-abroad-medical-influences-18th-century. Accessed 7 December 2023.

T, Milan, and Ellen Castelow. "Sir Walter Scott, his Life and Works." *Historic UK,* https://www.historic-uk.com/HistoryUK/HistoryofScotland/Sir-Walter-Scott/. Accessed 4 December 2023.

"WW1 Battalions." *The Royal Scots,* https://www.theroyalscots.co.uk/ww1-battalions/. Accessed 12 December 2023.

Printed in Great Britain
by Amazon

47418908R00056